T0157412

Smarten Up!

Why should you *Marry by Choice, Not by Chance*?
In the last century, marriage rates in the U.S. have hit
an all-time low, while the average age women get married
for the first time is at an all-time high.

If getting married and having children are primary components
of your life plan for happiness, *now* is the time to act. You should
be investing *at least* as much time, effort, and energy into those
goals as you are in creating your other successes.

SINCE WHEN HAVE SMART GIRLS WHO ASPIRE TO MARRIAGE AND MOTHERHOOD BEEN SEEN AS SOCIAL DEVIANTS?

Marry by Choice, Not by Chance is about empowering young
women to take responsibility—for themselves, their
happiness, their success, and their safety.

YOU ARE THE ARCHITECT OF YOUR LIFE.

Clearly, this advice isn't for everyone. If you are
all about your career—and only your career—then
this book probably isn't for you. But if you know that you
someday want to be married and have children, read
Marry by Choice, Not by Chance before it's too late.

What are people saying about
Susan Patton, aka "The Princeton Mom,"
and *MARRY BY CHOICE, NOT BY CHANCE*
(previously published as *Marry Smart*)?

"Like a trip to the car wash, where the dust of antagonistic feminist doctrine about sex and marriage gets blasted off the windshield so [young women] can see clearly."

—Charlotte Allen, *THE WALL STREET JOURNAL*

"For some of us, our personal and professional happiness are intertwined. But for those women for whom it's not, well, you should buy Patton's book and not be embarrassed to do so, regardless of what some of my fellow feminists may think."

—Keli Goff, *THE DAILY BEAST*

"Patton's message doesn't sound all that nuts. Why are we so reluctant to admit that it *is* hard to find eligible men (and women?) to marry? Why are people afraid to admit that, OK, the world of dating is sometimes thrilling and fun . . . but quite often, horrible and lonely? What's wrong with wanting to meet someone in college, presumably someone with whom you have shared experiences and stuff in common, and opt out of dealing with the crappy dates, the mystery texts, and the questioning looks from Auntie Mildred at the Thanksgiving table? And more to the point: *What's wrong with wanting to be happy, sooner?*"

—Kara Baskin, *BOSTON GLOBE*

"The Princeton Mom is Right. . . . The startling news is clear. The new feminist crisis is clear. One in five women who want to become mothers are being denied the freedom because they can't find a partner on time. There's a unique partner crunch at this time in history, because America is producing more successful women than men. And women are holding on to their anthropological instincts to marry a man who can provide."

—DR. WENDY WALSH, on her blog

"A spectacular human being. . . . I loved the book. Very readable. . . . What a terrific lady, articulate, strong."

—DR. LAURA SCHLESSINGER, on *Dr. Laura*

"Patton's deepest desire . . . is for women to be happy. She believes, like almost every Jewish mother I have ever met, that marriage and kids will make them just that. I agree with Patton's end goal."

—Elissa Strauss, *JEWISH DAILY FORWARD*

"Patton's advice . . . is sensible."

—Naomi Schaefer Riley, *NEW YORK POST*

"Susan Patton is in her prime."

—Maureen O'Connor, *NEW YORK*

"I'm on Team Patton. Let's not kid ourselves: being single sucks!"

—Amanda Lauren, *XOJANE*

Marry by Choice, Not by Chance

Marry by Choice, Not by Chance

Advice for Finding the Right One at the Right Time

Previously published as *Marry Smart*

Susan Patton

(aka "The Princeton Mom")

G

GALLERY BOOKS

New York London Toronto Sydney New Delhi

Gallery Books
A Division of Simon & Schuster, Inc.
1230 Avenue of the Americas
New York, NY 10020

Copyright © 2014 by Susan Patton

Previously published as *Marry Smart*

All rights reserved, including the right to reproduce this book or portions thereof in any form whatsoever. For information, address Gallery Books Subsidiary Rights Department, 1230 Avenue of the Americas, New York, NY 10020.

First Gallery Books paperback edition September 2014

GALLERY BOOKS and colophon are registered trademarks of Simon & Schuster, Inc.

For information about special discounts for bulk purchases,
please contact Simon & Schuster Special Sales at 1-866-506-1949
or business@simonandschuster.com.

The Simon & Schuster Speakers Bureau can bring authors to your live event.
For more information or to book an event, contact the Simon & Schuster Speakers Bureau at 1-866-248-3049 or visit our website at www.simonspeakers.com.

Interior design by Davina Mock-Maniscalco
Jacket design by Backscatter Graphics
Jacket photograph by Anthony Bradshaw/Getty Images

Manufactured in the United States of America

10   9   8   7   6   5   4   3   2

Library of Congress Cataloging-in-Publication Data

Patton, Susan, 1955–
    Marry smart : advice for finding the one / Susan Patton (a.k.a. "The Princeton Mom")—First Gallery Books hardcover edition 2014.
        pages   cm
    1. Mate selection—Humor.   2. Marriage—Humor.   3. Women—Conduct of life.
4. Women—Psychology—Popular works.   I. Title.
    HQ801.P3425 2014
    306.82—dc23   2013047238

ISBN 978-1-4767-5970-8
ISBN 978-1-4767-5971-5 (pbk)
ISBN 978-1-4767-5972-2 (ebook)

For my sons
And for all the daughters of Old Nassau
past, present, and future

Contents

PART II

....

YOUR TWENTIES

PART III

YOUR THIRTIES

PART IV

FIRST FIND YOURSELF. THEN FIND THE ONE

PART V

WISE ADVICE FOR WISE WOMEN

Introduction to the
Paperback Edition

$\mathscr{I}$T SEEMS I STRUCK A NERVE.

In the past few months, I've been called names that are so off base that I keep looking behind me, thinking that they must be talking about someone else. "Crazy." "Retrograde." "Elitist." "Stupid." "Evil." I'm really none of those things, but I understand that when you're in the public eye and people disagree with you passionately, they will throw everything they've got at you. It's okay. I'm a tough gal. The hysteria, the name-calling, the vitriol all point to the fact that this is a conversation that has been suppressed for far too long and very much needed to be initiated.

Everybody has an opinion about dating, mating, marriage, and motherhood, and now people are talking about these taboo topics. I've heard from friends I knew in elementary school, people I haven't thought of in fifty years; friends from middle school in the Bronx; clients and candidates I'd long lost touch with; Princeton acquaintances I've never seen at reunions. And I've made many new friends—people who contacted me to share their views about planning for personal happiness and send me links to relevant articles and videos. I've gotten to know journalists, broadcasters, television producers, network executives, radio programmers, publicity people, and the green room of every major broadcast studio in New York and elsewhere. (There is a distinct correlation between the quality of a program and the sumptuousness of their green-room snacks).

And being nominated for the *Time* 100 was an honor, as they say, just to be nominated.

So why has my book generated such extreme responses? I suppose that when you challenge several generations of conventional wisdom, it gets people talking—and that's good. My intent has always been to start a conversation that encourages young women to think about what they really want, and plan strategically for their future.

What is so outrageous about telling young women who aspire to marriage and motherhood to plan for their personal happiness sooner rather than later? With the aggressive marketing of extreme options to overcome age-based infertility, doesn't it make sense to remind young women that they have a limited window of opportunity to bear their own children—and that in terms of their fertility, forty is *not* the new thirty? And isn't it just common sense to suggest that they take advantage of their best chance to connect with the age-appropriate, single, like-minded young men . . . their classmates? Depending on where you are in your life, these things can be hard to hear.

Perhaps for some, my words hit a little too close to home.

At the core of this book is a message of empowerment that comes from taking personal responsibility—for yourself, your happiness, your success, and your safety. It's important to remind young women that they aren't the victims of their lives, but the architects. They can have professional success as well as domestic bliss if they plan for all of it wisely.

Perhaps the most outraged criticism of me was for my comments about personal responsibility. But I believe that at a time when violent assault on campus is an all-too-frequent occurrence, personal responsibility is a vital key to risk prevention. To suggest that young women bear little or no responsibility for their own safety is illogical, irresponsible, and dangerous. Women must be mindful of the visual and behavioral signals they are sending and not get so drunk or stoned that they can't get out of a social situation that is headed south. For their own safety, they must be in control of themselves. I'm not blaming victims of violent crimes—I'm saying *don't be a victim*!

Being in control means taking responsibility, staying safe, planning thoughtfully, keeping focused and listening to our inner selves to pursue what we really want in our lives . . . even if that includes the traditional roles of wife and mother.

Clearly, my advice isn't for everyone. If you are all about your career—and only your career—then this book probably isn't for you. But if you know that you *someday* want to be married and have children, you'd be wise to take my advice and start planning for this sooner rather than later. I'm not stating facts based on opinion, but opinions based on my observations as an experienced, well-educated woman, a mother, and human resources professional.

And again, it's just advice. Take it or leave it!

It is not surprising that so much of the *public* response has been critical. Those who agree with me simply don't have the same need to be outspoken as those who disagree with me.

The *private* responses that I have received from hundreds of young women, young men, parents of teenagers, grown women coping with regret and wishing this advice was given to them decades ago, and so many others have been truly heartwarming and validating. I appreciate the many feminist moms and progressive dads who quietly assure me that they have been sharing this same wise advice with their young daughters for years. They're afraid to say it out loud for fear of being attacked by the liberal-thinking groups that are all about diversity . . . except ideological diversity. If you think differently than they do, then they are completely intolerant and often nasty. I understand that the need to stay out of the firing line and be seen as politically correct remains overwhelming for many.

I smile to think about how many television interviewers leaned in to me just before (or after) our segment and whispered something like "I totally agree with everything you say, but you know that I have to go after you, right?"

Yes, I know.

Even the ultraliberal Jon Stewart, who lampooned me unmercifully on *The Daily Show*—and, honestly, what could be more flattering than being lampooned by Jon Stewart?—displayed my book prominently for more than eight minutes on his twenty-two-minute national broadcast. Despite his entertaining protest, I wouldn't be surprised if he had a copy of this book put aside for his young daughter.

A more media-savvy person might have anticipated the backlash and personal attacks, because that's just the way anonymous commentary and social media work. They could have predicted that my broader positions would be condensed and contorted into sound bites that make little sense out of context. But the vitriol surprised me. I did not expect such screaming outrage—and much of it, frankly, is faux outrage. There are groups and individuals who feel their agenda has not been given adequate attention, so they decided to distort my message for the sake of drawing attention to their own underappreciated causes. There's been a lot of parsing of words and playing of semantic games when the truth is that we all want the same thing—for young people to be happy, to be healthy, to pursue their goals and dreams in the best possible way, and to act responsibly. I've just put those thoughts in terms that are more straightforward—and less politically correct—than most people are willing to own.

Some people crave celebrity. I never have. I value my privacy and the ability to run out to the supermarket or the post office in sweatpants and without makeup. Being recognized by strangers is an unexpected and dizzying experience. It's forced me to up my game in terms of what I look like when I leave my apartment, which isn't a bad thing—and, honestly, a little bit of fame is fun!

I'm all for planning, but you can't plan for things that you can't even imagine. I hoped that my book would generate some attention and encourage young women to plan for their personal happiness, but the incredible response and controversy it created was more intense than anyone could have predicted.

Has all the critical commentary made me reconsider my thinking and change my opinions?

Nope, far from it. It's reinforced them!

Who Am I and
What Was I Thinking?

*S*O I WROTE A LETTER.

A letter to the editor of the newspaper of the college I attended forty years ago.

I wrote the letter because I was on campus for a Women and Leadership conference that was followed by a breakout session. This afforded current female undergraduates an opportunity to speak informally with alumnae. There were eight young women at my table and they were told that I am a human resources professional and an executive coach, so naturally we all chatted about career planning, resume writing, and interview techniques. Their eyes seemed to glaze over from yet again hearing still more advice about how to succeed in the working world.

Then I looked at each of them and asked, "Do any of you girls want to someday get married and have children?" Their jaws dropped. They were stunned by the very question. They looked cautiously at each other before sheepishly raising their hands. All eight aspired to marriage and motherhood—but not one of them wanted to admit it.

Now it was my turn to be stunned. These amazing young women

were reluctant to share their heartfelt hopes, for fear of critical judgment. It was clear to me that someone had to talk with them honestly about finding husbands, getting married, and having babies.

That someone might as well be me.

So I decided to write a letter to the editor, addressed to the daughters I never had. Back when I was an undergraduate, a proud member of one of the pioneering first classes of women to graduate from Princeton University, I dated but I never had a serious boyfriend. Instead of looking for and possibly finding a life partner among my college classmates, I spent almost ten years after college dating men who weren't as interesting, educated, or accomplished as my classmates had been. I ultimately married the man I had been dating for years, because if I was to fulfill my lifelong dream of having children, time was running out. He wasn't the love of my life, but we marry for many reasons. Sometimes, we make sacrifices to achieve our greater goals. I married at thirty-one years old because I knew that I wanted to have children and do so in a traditional marriage—and I was cognizant of the limitations on my ability to procreate. And although after twenty-five years my marriage ended in divorce, I consider it to have been successful—because I had the children I always wanted.

In retrospect, I realize that I may have squandered some of my best years looking for what I probably could have found as a student on campus when I was twenty years old. I wish somebody had told me when I was an undergraduate that I should look more carefully at my male classmates. There must have been many marriageable men in that group. Either I didn't recognize them, or I carelessly dismissed them for superficial reasons, or I allowed myself to be shouted down by feminists who made me feel that it was a betrayal to the sisterhood for an educated woman to be so interested in marriage.

Did the fact that I didn't choose a man with comparable academic credentials damage my marriage and contribute to my divorce? I don't know for sure. But I know it didn't help.

During my four years on campus, I did many things right. I made great friends, had wonderful experiences that I'll remember always, and I graduated! But there are at least as many things I wish I had done differently. I especially wish that I had had sense enough to look for a husband on campus before I graduated.

So I wrote a letter, and it went, as they say, "viral." Honestly, I thought I would just share a few words of simple, maternal advice with the girls on campus, where my younger son was an undergraduate. I didn't mean to cause an international firestorm or infuriate some women on campus, let alone on the Internet.

(Well, maybe I did expect a little controversy—I am more blunt than most people, I've always been like that—but who knew anyone would pay attention?)

And viral? Who thinks of going viral? Within three days of the publication of my letter to the editor of the *Daily Princetonian*, my advice exceeded 100 million inquiries on Google worldwide. Not all of the responses were positive. In fact, I was called "retro," "crazy," "a throwback"—and those are some of the nicer epithets. I was accused of being a traitor to feminism, a traitor to coeducation, and an elitist.

Somewhere early on in the brouhaha, I was dubbed the "Princeton Mom." And you know what? I love that moniker! I earned it, both by graduating from Princeton and by having two children who went there. The advice I offered in the *Daily Princetonian* was intended for the women on the campus of my beloved alma mater, but it is applicable to smart women everywhere who want a traditional family. To avoid a life of unwanted spinsterhood—with cats!—you have to smarten up about what's important to you, and keep your head in the game. You have to plan for your personal happiness with the same commitment and dedication that you plan for your professional success.

Honestly, what about that is so controversial?

Knowing and respecting yourself. That's what it's really about: understanding what's important to you and prioritizing. That's what it's about. When I say, "Find a man," what I really mean is "Find a man who will respect you." And when I say, "Find a husband in college," what I'm really saying is "It's never too early to start planning for your personal happiness and looking for a husband who will respect you."

It's never too early, and it's never too late. (Well, that's not really true, but we'll discuss that later.)

So, with the benefit of hindsight, this book contains the advice I wish I had been given when I was younger, which I now offer to educated young women everywhere.

I KNOW TOO MANY BRILLIANT, successful women who invest too many years in developing *only* their career. They reach their thirties and realize that it's almost impossible to find a suitable husband—*the one!*—especially with their biological clocks ticking louder and faster every year. Many of them wind up single and miss their opportunity for motherhood. And you know what? No corporate achievement, impressive title, or astronomical salary can ever compensate a woman who learns that she's waited too long and can no longer bear her own children.

I've worked in human resources for decades, as a consultant to media businesses as well as an executive coach to senior-level executives, primarily in magazine publishing, advertising, marketing, and digital properties. Most of my clients and candidates are women, because historically, the publishing industry has employed an inordinately large number of women. Perhaps that's because it is a *soft* business that doesn't usually require a lot of math or science, but more likely because it doesn't pay very well, so men are usually compelled to look elsewhere for better-salaried positions. As an executive coach, I frequently hear from women who are at the pinnacle of their careers. They are senior vice presidents, executive vice presidents, publishers, editors in chief, earning relatively huge six-figure salaries; some have virtually unlimited travel and entertainment budgets. Many even have a significant wardrobe allowance, because they work in a fashion industry and are required to look . . . fashionable.

These women call me expressing an odd sense of dissatisfaction, presumably looking for guidance in identifying their next best opportunity. We talk and they tell me that they still love the property they work for, that they continue to feel respected by their management and supported by their staff, and that they are very well compensated. So what's the problem? A job change is unlikely to improve their already outstanding situation. So I ask them to remind me of how old they are, even though I know they are in their mid-thirties. I ask if they are married (even though I know that they are not). Do they have any prospects? No, they answer, not really. These women are truly accomplished, respected professionals, each at the top of her game, but they are all profoundly unhappy.

They had found out that you can't have it all when all you have is your work.

So, I wanted to offer *balanced* advice to the young women at my son's college.

What, you may ask (as many on the Internet have), qualifies me to offer these suggestions? My answer is "the same things that qualify anyone to offer personal advice": nothing more than life experience, keen observation, and the desire to be helpful. Let me say that, as with any advice, it isn't applicable to everyone, and it certainly isn't intended to be critical of anyone (even though I sound like that sometimes). It might be useful for women who know that someday they will want to have their own children and to do so in something resembling a traditional marriage, and it might be useful for women who are thinking about how to best plan for their personal happiness.

If you are neither, this book may aggravate you as much as my letter did!

There are very few statistics in this book, and my research has been limited to talking with people I know, like, and trust—many of whom hold very different opinions from my own. In almost every chapter, I've tried to include anecdotes and some personal history that is intended to provide context for how my opinions were informed. Some chapters address very serious issues, and others are lighthearted. My intent is not to provoke anger, but instead to inspire a dialogue that has been too long suppressed. No doubt some of these words will incur the angry response of anonymous bloggers, and those who consider me some kind of antifeminist. That's okay . . . it's only words, not sticks and stones.

And I'm a pretty tough gal.

You see, you live long enough and certain truths become clear. Some of the things that we come to understand in our fifties would have been inconceivable in our twenties. Young women today want many of the same things that young women have always wanted . . . and more. Such a broad range of professional and educational opportunities weren't always available to women of previous generations, and for these new possibilities all women are appreciative. But along the path toward these enhanced choices, some women have lost sight of their oldest and most basic goals—finding a husband and having children. They certainly want family, but the zeitgeist for educated young women has turned them away from pursuing any kind of a traditional courtship.

I sincerely believe that young women need *better* advice than they are being given. I encourage *every* young woman to take advantage of *every* new opportunity . . . but maybe not at the expense of one of our oldest and most fundamental dreams.

So if marriage and children are important to you, make them every bit as important as professional success and achievement.

If you don't want to have children and you don't want to be married, then don't bother reading this book. Much of this advice won't apply to you.

I think you know *exactly* what I'm talking about.

You have known it for years, actually, only somewhere along the way you stopped listening to yourself, or maybe you were shouted down by people or groups promoting their own agenda—not yours. Or maybe you decided to be politically correct instead of standing up for what you *really* want.

Smarten up, girl!

You may aspire to corporate leadership or professional status, but at what cost? At the end of the day, will you be satisfied with coming home to another stack of financial reports or spending another long night reviewing company documents?

If you think you won't, *smarten up*!

If getting married and having children are primary components of your life plan for happiness, this book will encourage you to invest at *least* as much time, effort, and energy in developing your personal happiness as you do in planning for your professional success. In fact, figuring out how to achieve your personal happiness needs much more of your attention—and the process should start sooner than you think. By the time you graduate from college, almost half of your childbearing years will be behind you. Yes, I know that everyone has a friend who has an older sister who had a baby in her mid-forties, but that is an exception to the rule. You know that, don't you?

By your mid-thirties, your best childbearing years are over.

And so are your best chances for finding THE ONE.

This book contains my personal opinions, based on my personal experience and observation. I don't expect everyone to agree with me, nor do I require a chorus of experts to support my thinking.

It's just advice . . . take it or leave it!

PART I

Your College Years

My advice is applicable to smart women everywhere: Make the most of your college years. The uniqueness of your college experience may not be evident to you until long after you graduate, but trust me . . . it is the most extraordinary time. Use it to your very best advantage. Put in place the components of your life plan for happiness. Get the best education you can, explore your passions and interests, develop a work ethic that makes you proud, establish lasting friendships, and look around for a potential life partner—you'll never have a better opportunity to do so.

Remember that if you use your time on campus wisely, they will not have been the best four years of your life. They will be only the beginning of the best years of your life.

The Letter

March 29, 2013

Advice for the Young Women of Princeton—
the Daughters I Never Had

Forget about having it all, or not having it all, leaning in or
leaning out . . . here's what you really need to know that nobody
is telling you.

For years (decades, really) we have been bombarded with advice
on professional advancement, breaking through that glass ceiling
and achieving work-life balance. We can figure that out—we are
Princeton women. If anyone can overcome professional obstacles,
it will be our brilliant, resourceful, very well educated selves.

When I was an undergraduate in the mid-seventies, the two
hundred pioneer women in my class would talk about navigating
the virile plains of Princeton as a precursor to professional success.
Never being one to shy away from expressing an unpopular
opinion, I said that I wanted to get married and have children.
It was seen as heresy.

For most of you, the cornerstone of your future and happiness will be inextricably linked to the man you marry, and you will never again have this concentration of men who are worthy of you.

Here's what nobody is telling you . . . find a husband on campus before you graduate.

Yes, I went there.

Men regularly marry women who are younger, less intelligent, less educated. It's amazing how forgiving men can be about a woman's lack of erudition, if she is exceptionally pretty. Smart women can't (shouldn't) marry men who aren't at least their intellectual equals. As Princeton women, we have almost priced ourselves out of the market. Simply put, there is a very limited population of men who are as smart or smarter than we are. And I say again—you will never again be surrounded by this concentration of men who are worthy of you.

Of course, once you graduate you will meet men who are your intellectual equal—just not that many of them. And, you could choose to marry a man who has other things to recommend him besides a soaring intellect. But ultimately, it will frustrate you to be with a man who just isn't as smart as you.

Here is another truth that you know, but nobody is talking about. As freshman women, you have four classes of men to choose from. Every year, you lose the men in the senior class, and are older than the class of incoming freshman men. So, by the time you are a senior, you basically have only the men in your own class to choose from, and frankly—they now have four classes of women to choose from. Maybe you should have been a little nicer to these guys when you were freshmen?

If I had daughters, this is what I would be telling them.

—Susan A. Patton, Class of 1977

It's Harder for Us Smart Women

*I*F YOU ARE A WELL-EDUCATED WOMAN HOPING TO MARRY A MAN WHO is at least your intellectual equal, you have almost priced yourself out of the market. Honestly, where do you think that you will find super-smart men once you are no longer a student? At a bar? Online? You know that the men on your campus are just as smart as you are—they got into the same school that you did! They take the same classes. You see them in the library, pulling all-nighters studying, taking exams. Once you enter the *real* world, you'll be stunned by how smart the men are . . . not. In fact, the collective erudition of *most* of the people you meet (men and women) out of an academic environment will distinctly disappoint you. They may have many other things to recommend them, but it will probably be a mistake to attempt to engage most of them in the kind of serious discussions about esoteric subjects you can chat about in college. After all, 22 percent of the American public believe that Elvis is still alive.

You don't *have* to marry a man who is as smart, capable, and accomplished as you . . . but tell the truth: Don't you want to? Clearly, your admission to college was not by accident. You've invested yourself in academic achievement, and your discipline, hard work, and character are what earned you a place at that institution you are justly proud of. Of course you want a husband who shares those values and that work ethic. You'll find *some* of these men after you graduate, but you'll never again have this many wonderful men who are single and age-appropriate to choose from as you do on your college campus.

Can you be happily married to a man who isn't as smart as you? It depends on what you want from marriage. If your priority is financial security, a huge bank account may be enough to satisfy you. And then of course, there are some very self-sufficient women who marry slightly unintelligent, ultra-studly men just for the sex. Okay, but the likelihood is that after a while even the most Thrilling Circus Sex with Mr. Macho will become Mechanical Boring Sex with Annoying Dumb Guy. And that's not something that's likely to get better. The sex won't improve and he definitely won't ever get smarter.

The *big* thing is that you want to form a lifelong union with a man who will celebrate and encourage your achievements and never be threatened by your capacity for greatness, simply because he has a similar track record and those same capacities. But it's the *little* things that continue to surface that will remind you of why you should marry a smart man. You will either have to regularly explain your references to things like Fermat's Last Theorem or Diaghilev or the Bayeux Tapestry—or else get used to that glazed look that comes over his face when he just doesn't get it. There is a wonderful scene in the movie *Swingers* where Mike (Jon Favreau's character) tries to impress a waitress in a Las Vegas diner. The menu says, "We serve breakfast any time." He asks her for an omelet in the Age of Enlightenment. The waitress walks away in disgust and Mike rues having used a time frame that was "over her head," and wishes he referenced the more commonly known Renaissance. A few minutes later, the waitress returns with his order and says, "Here's your eggs, Voltaire."

Okay, so Mike underestimated the woman's intellectual prowess, but if *your* date doesn't understand why this is funny, he's not smart enough for you.

Beyond your frustration at his not getting cultural references, you will want a man who can express himself as elegantly and as eloquently as you can. Command of the English language is important, and a limited vocabulary, bad grammar, and the inability to construct a proper sentence will drive you crazy. It is comical to watch Meadow Soprano's reaction to her uneducated boyfriend Jackie Aprile Jr.'s objection when he thinks she is using a Spanish word in their Scrabble game. If your man doesn't recognize *oblique* as a proper English word, you won't think that is at all funny.

While some men might find it adorable that their little wife doesn't know about high finances, or global perspectives in government and politics, you will *not* experience making excuses for your husband as in any way adorable. And neither will he. The chances are that he is smart enough to know that he isn't smart enough for you. Recognizing that you and your friends know things that he doesn't, he may ask you to buy him a copy of *Ulysses* or *The Fountainhead*. But he'll never actually read them, and probably wouldn't understand them if he did.

Most men's egos are fragile. If you can imagine the stress that is associated with your being smarter than he is, just think about what will happen when you outearn him, which, unless you purposefully hold yourself back, you probably will.

Smart Advice

- Look for a man who will celebrate and encourage your achievements.

- Look for a man who will not be threatened by your capacity for greatness.

- Beware of marrying a dumb guy for good sex: The sex won't improve and he'll never get smarter.

Marriage and Motherhood: The Modern Taboo

$\mathcal{S}$INCE WHEN HAVE SMART GIRLS WHO ASPIRE TO MARRIAGE AND motherhood been seen as social deviants? Why are these women disrespected by those who say they have betrayed themselves and the *sisterhood*, and that they have squandered their education? There is absolutely nothing mutually exclusive about women being well educated *and* aspiring to marriage and motherhood. And there is little that will better prepare you for the challenges of raising a family than a good education.

For all the things that change over time and are modernized and mechanized, some things stay the same. The dream of domestic bliss remains a constant for most smart girls. I understand that marriage is not for all women, nor is motherhood on every woman's bucket list. But the majority of women I know most certainly consider a husband and children as essential components in their life plan for happiness.

Here's something else that hasn't changed in forty years: the scorn that these girls endure if they are courageous enough to say that they want these traditional elements of domestic life. When I was an undergraduate in the 1970s, I most certainly was interested in finding a man who would be a good husband and father. When I would share that dream with classmates (both men and women . . . but mostly women), they looked at me like I was crazy. It seemed to many that domesticity was inconsistent with what a well-educated woman should want. I was frequently asked why I would consider "throwing away" a Princeton education on "raising a family." I couldn't understand why pursuing the latter was the equivalent of discarding the former. I didn't think I was at Princeton to develop skills that would necessarily empower me to rule the world. I thought I was there to get the best possible education to put to use living the best possible life—however I chose to define that life for myself.

I always believed that having an outstanding education would be important in creating a home and bringing up children, but as an undergraduate I couldn't have imagined exactly how important it would be. With the benefit of years of experience, hindsight, and having raised two spectacular sons, let me assure you that excellent schooling is the best path to a full life of attractive options, and a tremendous asset in raising a family. Your exceptional academic credentials provide the daily example that you set for your children as to the value of learning, intellectual curiosity, and personal achievement. These are the things that you want them to own, because these are the things that will expand your children's options and keep them engaged and inspired for a lifetime.

I've heard the case made for how women who would choose to stay at home and raise children should be denied places in the best educational institutions in favor of women who will use their degree in some broader way. I couldn't disagree more! Admission should be based on demonstrated achievement, ability to handle academic work, and potential for contributing to campus life. It should not be quid pro quo for—

or predicated upon—the promise of what you will do with the degree once you earn it. Admission to the best universities has become so intensely competitive that anyone admitted to these esteemed institutions has certainly earned their "fat envelope" through distinguished performance and personal dedication. Whether you intend to run a business, lead a country, rule the world, or raise a family, your superb education will help you in pursuing *all* that you want for yourself.

Regardless of how taboo marriage and motherhood may be in your circle of friends, if it's what you want, you'll have to shake off the cynics in order to own it proudly. You're going to have to put just as much care and attention toward satisfying your maternal instinct as you would toward satisfying your need for the next promotion at work. And make no mistake, your education and cognitive skills will be put to use every day of your marriage (of your life, really) and in facing the challenges of raising children well. Your kids will see you as their own personal Oracle of Delphi. They will expect you to know everything. Don't disappoint them.

If marriage and motherhood are authentic to who you are, embrace it, welcome it, and find a good man who will realize this dream with you.

Even the most successful, accomplished women will say that there is nothing that they are prouder of, or that is more meaningful to them than having had their families. It's a special dream that many women hold and earnestly pray for. But they have stopped listening to their inner selves. Marriage and motherhood have become thought of by some as the antithesis of modern womanhood, instead of as the essential components they have always been and will always be.

Many intelligent young women need to be reminded that carrying a bouquet down the aisle can be a good thing and holding a baby in your arms can feel like the best thing you'll ever do. For many of you, marriage to the right man will fill your hearts and define the arc of your lives. And for many of you, the joy of giving birth and raising children will be the pinnacle of your life's happiness.

Taboo? Absolutely not!

Smart Advice

- Being well educated and wanting marriage and motherhood are not mutually exclusive.
- If getting married and being a mother is important to you, embrace it, welcome it, and find a good man who will realize this dream with you.
- If getting married and being a mother is important to you, work as hard toward satisfying your maternal instinct as you would toward satisfying your need for the next promotion.

Look for the Good Boys— They Grow into the Good Men

*L*ISTEN, GIRLS, JUST RESIST THE TEMPTATION TO DATE THE BAD BOYS or the crazy boys. Mostly because they are bad and crazy, but also because it's not good for your heart, your head, your soul, or your body to give yourself to a man you know isn't good for you.

I don't understand what masochistic mechanism kicks in that propels good women into the arms of bad men. But almost all women would have to admit to at some point having dated a loser, a snake, a moron, or a sexy bad boy. Sadly, many women don't smarten up soon enough and wind up marrying them. I was recently addressing a group of women in Philadelphia and the very gracious hostess had cocktail napkins on the table that read "She could no longer pretend that he wasn't an idiot." I liked these napkins so much that (with the hostess's permission, of course) I took several of them home and framed one to hang in my living room. What woman doesn't at some time in the course of dating the wrong man—or, worse yet, being married to him—think this?

You know better. Don't waste your time or yourself on men who, simply put, aren't worthy of you.

Who are the men who are worthy? Look around at the guys in your classes, maybe even the shy ones. The awkward ones, the guys who will never be *players*, the ones who will probably grow up to be great men of substance and accomplishment. They're not the cool guys right now, but they're likely to be the ones who will be the most successful. They're the ones who will probably be the best husbands and fathers. They're the ones who will ultimately make you much happier than the selfish, cocky BMOCs.

It is my observation that men don't seem to have a problem being with women who are dumb, mean, or nasty—if the women are pretty and willing to have sex with them. In fact, many men *love* to be with nasty girls. And when I say "be with," I mean "have sex with." They can take their time and date all kinds of women over many decades before settling down and starting a family. Men know that they won't marry these terrible women, but they also know that their future wife may very well demand monogamy, so they had better sow their wild oats while they can. Women don't have anywhere near as many years to experiment with men, especially with men they know they wouldn't marry even if you held a gun to their head. If you are going to have children before your ovarian shelf life leaves you with powdered eggs, you can't waste time with unmarriageable men.

We all talk about wanting to find nice guys, good men who are sweet, sensitive, and caring, but with remarkable frequency too many of us wind up with just the opposite. So why are we attracted to these bad boys? Is it just the promise of hot sex? Or do we think that we can convert them? Show them the way to be better men? *Inspire* them to become better men? The truth is, we can't convert them and they won't change. The egomaniacal, self-serving, unreliable, financially unstable, or commitment-phobic jerk whom you think you can fix has probably been hardwired to be that way since long before you met him.

Our mission to civilize is wasted on these bad boys.

Move on.

It is particularly off-putting when older women suggest that girls be almost reckless in whom they sleep with before marriage, so that they can experience a broad spectrum of men before they hunker down and become wives and mothers.

This is terrible advice.

Women can't and shouldn't date with the carelessness that men do. Because of the way it is designed, the female body is a receptacle for all sorts of diseases that men escape. Not being a doctor or psychiatrist, I don't know how to quantify women's physiological or psychological response to sex, but I know enough to know that it is different from men's response. I remember hearing a famous broadcast journalist (and notorious womanizer) define "Eternity" as "the time after you come and she goes." When men have completed the act, they are done. Women can bask in the afterglow almost indefinitely.

It's possible that men occasionally feel used by women for sex, but it's usually the other way around. Women have to be more careful about the men they are with. When grown women with children of their own tell young girls to date all kinds of men—even the ones they know aren't right for them—it sounds like they are either trying to escape their own boredom by living vicariously through these girls or they are desperately seeking to appear *hip*. It reminds me of parents who thought their teenagers would look more favorably upon them if they underwrote their marijuana purchases—or even worse, joined their kid's circle of friends and had a toke on the joint that was being passed around.

And while we're on the subject, *don't date married men!*

You deserve to be more than a mistress, a side squeeze, a paramour. Why should you settle for being the "other woman" in a clandestine relationship? Yes, I understand that he is probably lavishing attention on you because he is unhappy at home. Yes, I understand that his wife doesn't understand him. Or does she? Maybe she understands all too well that he is a selfish pig who has no respect for her or for their marital vows. Even if he leaves his wife and says that he'll marry you (which he won't, okay?), you must understand that if he would cheat *with* you, he will most certainly cheat *on* you.

Allow me to repeat myself: If he cheats *with* you, he will also cheat *on* you.

Again, move on.

Think twice before marrying a divorced man with children. Doing so could easily be what my mother would describe as "getting into a sickbed with a healthy head." Okay, so if you're older and past the time that you can bear your own children, then maybe this isn't such a bad idea, but if you are a young woman with childbearing years in front of you, be very careful about taking on the responsibility and challenges of children who aren't yours and the inevitable baggage that comes with a man who's been divorced.

In your early twenties, you are the most prized of all women. It's important that you remember you are first quality in every way. Your partner/spouse/boyfriend should be an enhancement to your life, not a drain on it.

Smart Advice

- Bad boys grow up to be bad husbands and bad fathers.

- Don't waste your time or yourself on men who aren't worthy of you.

- Don't date married or unavailable men. You deserve to be more than a mistress.

- In your early twenties, you are at the height of your desirability. Set your sights high and use this time to your best advantage. The pickings may never be as good again.

The "Hookup" Culture

INCREASINGLY, ROMANTIC COURTSHIP HAS BEEN REPLACED BY casual sex. Young women have lost sight of their own worth and are missing out on some of life's great joys—flirting, dating, and falling in love.

The progression of a romantic relationship should *slowly* lead to intimacy. It can't start there. If it does, there is no place for the relationship to go. It crests too soon, and then it dies, leaving many women feeling used and empty. Research suggests that as many as three-quarters of American college students have engaged in casual sex. Apparently, only the first hookup is fraught with angst. Studies show that once a young woman has engaged in uncommitted sex, she is much more likely to continue to have meaningless sexual experiences. Once the initial hurdle of immorality is crossed without apparent consequence, repeating the bad behavior is all too easy.

How did we ever come to this? When did sex become impersonal and devalued? Perhaps in 1998, when President Clinton said, "I did not have sexual relations with that woman, Miss Lewinsky." Yes, he most certainly *did* have sex with that woman. The touching, fondling, and exploration of a woman's genitals—with or without a costly Montecristo—is definitely sex. Out of his own political necessity, the president declared that anything short of intercourse doesn't count as sex; it has no meaning and there are no consequences. The president's denial reset the definition and perception of what sex is and what sex isn't.

Without discussing cows and free milk, and trying not to pass judgment on the relative morality of casual sex, you need to be reminded that at best, this behavior poses risks to both your physical and mental health. How could meaningless sex not result in diminishing a young woman's self-esteem?

Wake up, girls!

I think that most young women know that casual sex is bad for them, and that there is nothing about hooking up that is empowering. It's demeaning, unbecoming, and the furthest thing from a demonstration of strength or liberation. The most empowered women and wives are those who are in committed relationships with wonderful men who respect them. True liberation comes from knowing that you always have a date on Saturday night, that there will be one special valentine for you every February 14, knowing exactly whom you'll be locking lips with on New Year's Eve, and that through thick and thin you have a partner for life.

If the overwhelming majority of women are engaging in hookups, the peer pressure for *all* women to do so must be significant. Men have certainly come to expect free sex and it's ridiculous to think that it will be the men who change the tide on this trend. When women stop making themselves so available to men without commitment, men might start thinking about serious relationships.

Competing with the *easy* girls is nothing new and has always been a challenge for the *good* girls. Every generation has had women who would rather be chased than chaste. When I came of age in the 1970s the birth control pill was widely available, and with the virtual guarantee of pregnancy-free sex, even some of the most virtuous young women were sometimes a little promiscuous. But they were discreet about it. There wasn't any currency associated with these casual encounters. They happened privately and mostly infrequently.

Of course, there were also a few women who everyone knew had been *around* more than the drum on a clothes dryer. They were easy to spot; they were overdone, wore too much makeup and flashy jewelry, and were flirtatious in ways that were obvious and unappealing. They quickly but transiently turned the heads of young men who surely didn't respect them but were absolutely interested in what they were offering. Some things never change.

How can you compete for the best men with women who *are* willing to hook up with them? The answer is that you can't, at least not in the short term. For men, there is very little that trumps free sex with a woman who is easier to make than a peanut butter sandwich. But don't be discouraged. The good men won't want to marry these girls. They will be very happy to have casual sex with them as long as it's available, but when they think about the women with whom they might want to make a home and have children, it won't be these women.

In one very important aspect, I think that young men dream about their future wives the same way that young women dream about their future husbands—as the *other* parent of their future children. Because they don't have a loudly ticking biological clock, men can take much more time to find the future mother of their children, but they most certainly think long term about the women they will eventually marry and who will bear the children they expect to someday have. Ask any college-aged man to describe his future wife. Even the most die-hard Casanova will provide a surprisingly poetic description. This description is wholly incompatible with a woman who is regularly engaging in casual sex. Yes, men think about marriage and fatherhood; they just don't have women's imperative to achieve either one before it's too late. Interestingly, because there are very different biological investments by each gender in the bringing forth of a child, men look at women more critically than women look at men in this regard. There is his two-minute sperm contribution, and then there is your nine months of gestation and sixteen hours of labor. When a man thinks about the woman who will someday give birth to his baby and nurse his newborn son or daughter, he gets positively dewy-eyed. This maternal vision is absolutely inconsistent with a girl who engages in hookups and casual sex.

Good men look for good women to be the future mother of their children. Of course, during their college years, most men aren't actively thinking about getting married. They are having too much fun with too many women to think about shutting down that gravy train. By the time they are in their mid- to late twenties, they are starting to think about settling down. This is why it is smart to stay in touch with the men you met on campus, long after graduation. They are prequalified good marriage material in that you've shared your college experience and know that they are of a comparable intellectual orientation. Scope them out while you're a student, date for as long as it takes, and when they reach the stage that they are ready to marry, you'll be in place and have the home court advantage.

Instead of uncommitted sexual encounters, you should want something better for yourself. You have to keep reminding yourself that you deserve it.

Smart Advice

- Potential buyers are unmotivated if offered free merchandise, i.e., it's the lonely cow that gives away free milk.

- Casual sex poses risks to your physical and mental health. Don't do it.

- Meaningful sex in a committed relationship is empowering. You deserve it.

- Whatever kind of sex you're having, be discreet about it.

Multitasking at College—
Do Every*thing*, Not Every*one*

$\mathcal{I}$F YOU'RE AN UNDERGRADUATE TODAY, YOU'VE LIKELY BEEN A STU-
dent your whole life, except for your first four or five years, which you
probably don't remember. For many of you, the true wonder of your college experience will become abundantly clear only years *after* graduation. Never again will you be surrounded by so many like-minded peers
who are your age and mostly single. Use your time on campus to do
everything: Get a world-class education, find your best friends (they'll be
with you for a lifetime), and look *seriously* at your classmates for potential life partners.

While you are a student, you or your parents are paying a lot of
money for you to be at school. Once you're in the working world, most
of your time will be paid for by others, which will dramatically cut down
on your ability to choose how you spend your time. Use these special college years to explore *all* of the things that are of interest to you, even if
only tangentially. You might never have another opportunity to dabble in
some of your more unconventional interests, and you may surprise yourself. Ballroom dancing? Try it. You might like it and could be very good
at it. And if you're lucky, you might meet a fabulous dancing partner!

I smile at the amazing scope of extracurricular activities on campuses today. The staples are just as they were when I was a student. You can write for the school newspaper, sing in an a cappella group, get involved in women's sports, or be the cheerleader who inspires the team. But the possibilities for involvement, enrichment, inspiration, and enjoyment are so much broader than that. Even the groups that were once reserved only for those with special talents are now available to *anyone* with an interest in participating.

For instance, joining the marching band used to require the ability to read music and play an instrument, but now anyone who can enthusiastically bang a trash can lid is welcome to join the garbage-can percussion section of most groups. Grab a lid and get in there! Nobody has more fun than the marching band. When I was a student, I spent more time singing and dancing at McCarter Theatre with the Princeton Triangle Club than I did in class. Triangle is an undergraduate theater group, founded by Booth Tarkington in 1891, that every year writes and performs an original musical comedy. Even the club members who couldn't really sing or dance had a great time shuffling from side to side in the back of the chorus.

If you are a musician of more classical training, join the orchestra, wind ensemble, or the oh-so-esoteric Georgian Chorus. For the more academically inclined, there are spoken language tables at most of the dining halls. I understand that Table Scandinavia is especially popular for its beautiful blond participants. Or maybe your university has an apiary club or an Ornithologist's Nest. Did you know that there is such a thing as a cheese club? Okay, why not bond over a lovely Camembert! If your special interest isn't represented on campus, start a club and recruit fellow enthusiasts. This is how you get to know people; it's how you meet your best friends and might meet the love of your life.

Every college campus has some form of religious life represented by

Hillel, evangelical fellowship, Chabad, Aquinas Institute, Hindu society, Islamic center, or some other, more general outlet for spiritual enrichment. I urge you to connect with other students on campus who share your religious beliefs. Chances are, you share much more than just that.

Meals on campus have always been a great time to catch up with friends and meet new ones. Get to breakfast occasionally. The people you'll meet over pancakes and eggs are different from the ones you'll meet over meat loaf and seafood Newburg. Take the opportunity of an open seat at an otherwise filled table to introduce yourself. You really don't need much more in common than the fact that you both go to the same school and know that today's Turkey Surprise was last week's roast turkey and tomorrow's turkey meatballs. Remember, you're not at college for the food.

And then there are the things that not only should you do at college, but you should *only* do at college, like improvisational comedy. Trust me, you're not as funny as you think you are. Try it on campus, get it out of your system, and move on.

Another thing you'll probably consider while you are a student is to test your own tolerance for alcohol. I truly don't like the excessive drinking that seems to be prevalent on college campuses, but I understand that students drink and that it is a way to relax, let loose, and get a little crazy. As much as I hope you will *not* drink to excess, if you are going to test your own limits, it's better to do so on campus, where there is an infrastructure to take care of you. After you graduate, getting stupidly tipsy at the office holiday party will be something that can seriously damage your professional reputation and harm your prospects for career advancement. It's a stupid thing to do, but at least overindulging at school will probably have fewer long-term repercussions. There are consequences, but depending on the severity of your inebriation, and the kindheartedness of the people around you, you might get off easy and have to deal only with your classmates reminding you at every re-union of the time that you were so drunk that you walked into the din-ing room wearing only socks and a smile.

When you are a freshman, every group on campus will want you to want to join them. Get on all of their mailing lists. Know what's going on. Attend events with good school spirit and an enthusiastic attitude. You'll attract positive attention, and in the right frame of mind, you'll probably have some fun. And you never know whom you'll meet!

I love sleeping and am a serious advocate for getting eight hours of shut-eye per night. However, you can't possibly do so while also doing everything else you want to do on campus—and your schoolwork. You have a lifetime to catch up on lost sleep. Once you graduate, you won't have the opportunity to explore all of this stuff.

Use your time at school to your very best advantage.

Smart Advice

- Use your time on campus to explore everything that interests you.
- Get involved in many activities, with enthusiasm, and broaden your network.
- Connect seriously with people who are interested in the same extracurricular activities as you, and remain connected after graduation.

So, Go Find a Husband Already!

"GATHER YE ROSEBUDS WHILE YE MAY" OR "YOU MAY FOREVER TARRY." Seventeenth-century English poet Robert Herrick was right, and so am I. Your best and most productive rosebud-gathering years are when you are at the cusp of adulthood, and the greatest concentration of outstanding rosebuds to gather will be found on your college or graduate school campus. Your meddling aunt is also right when she says, "What are you waiting for? You're not getting any younger."

I'm not necessarily advocating that you marry immediately upon graduation, unless of course you and your husband-to-be are ready to do so. I know many people who married within months of earning their college degree. They were young and in love and navigated those first years postgraduation together. You may not be ready to marry as soon as that, but you have to start seriously looking for your life partner *much* earlier than you may think.

While you are a student, start scoping out the men you might consider marrying—and then stay in touch with them! Date for as long as it takes until the time is right for you—but don't wait too long. You'll never be more attractive than you are as a very young woman, and if you hope to have children, remember that your fertility has distinct limitations. If that same meddlesome aunt is middle-aged and without children, there's a reason that she is reminding you that you're not getting any younger: She never did.

Let's face it: By the time you are thirty years old, your marriage prospects will have diminished dramatically from what they were when you were twenty. And when you're thirty and still hope to have children, a distinct panic will start to sets in. I wish it weren't so, but look around at your older sisters, cousins, friends, and coworkers. By your mid-thirties, the men whom you'd be most interested in marrying (successful men in their mid- to late thirties) are already married, often to women younger than you. They probably even have a baby or two at home. Wait a few more years and absolute desperation takes over and that has an effect not unlike giving off man-repellent. I'm not making this up. It's true.

I know. You're probably thinking that at twenty years old, you don't know who you'll be at thirty, so how can you search for a husband who will be appropriate for your more adult self?

The truth is that who you are at thirty is quite different than who you'll be at forty. And, when your children are grown and you are fully middle-aged, you will be a very different person at fifty than you were at forty. Life is a continuum. We are always growing and changing. You and a good spouse can evolve through the decades and hopefully grow *with* each other, and be supportive and comforting through all of life's ups and downs. The vicissitudes of aging are realities that all of us face. We can't predict who we will be as we mature, but finding a good spouse early and evolving as people together and growing old together is better than being alone. (I know. For *some* people.)

Sometime in the early 1990s, the median age of first marriage became higher than the median age of first births. Really, girls? Baby first, marriage later? Whatever happened to "First comes love, then comes marriage, *then* comes Susie with a baby carriage"? Having a baby in a traditional marriage with two parents is hard enough.

Raising a child on one income can be done—and done well—but it is not the easiest way to live your life, and it frequently saddles your baby with a disadvantage.

Find a good husband early—it's better for you, and better for your baby.

Smart Advice

- Start planning for your personal happiness sooner rather than later. It'll be later much sooner than you think.
- If you hope to have children, remember that your fertility has distinct limitations.
- Don't wait until panic sets in to start looking for a husband. Desperation is unattractive, and the clock is ticking.

Smart Is Sexy

*E*VERYONE SAYS THAT "PRETTY" IS SEXY, BUT YOU KNOW WHAT'S SEXY?

- Smart is sexy.

- Kind is sexy.

- Funny is sexy.

- Happy is sexy.

- Talented is sexy.

- Confident is sexy.

And here's a short list of what's not sexy:

- Overexposed lady parts is not sexy.

- Promiscuity is not sexy.

- Vulgarity is not sexy.

- Too much makeup is not sexy.

- Whining and complaining is not sexy.

- Insecurity is not sexy.

- Stupid is not sexy.

Attracting the best possible life partner is not unlike attracting the best possible buyer for a home you'd like to sell. When a house is put on the market it is cleaned up, flaws are repaired, the lawns are manicured, gardens are planted. In other words, everything is done to make it as attractive as possible for potential buyers. By your late teens and early twenties, you should be looking your very best if you want to attract the most desirable men. Yes, there is much more to you than your appearance, but initial attraction is superficial, so let's think about what you look like and how that helps or hurts you.

At your most attractive, you are also prepared to make the best use of your college experience. And on campus, you have the greatest concentration of wonderful men to consider as life partners. Do *everything* you can to look as good as possible by the time you get to college. If you are seriously overweight (you know if you are) or have stubby, nail-bitten fingers, take serious stock of yourself and make whatever alterations you can, so that you can reflect your best self. Physical attraction certainly isn't the best or most meaningful measure of a person, but it is undeniably the first measure by which potential mates are judged. I hope that you find men who will value you for the content of your character, but first you have to get their attention. And, even if the wonderful man you meet can happily see past your extra weight, his friends may not, and their ridicule won't work in your favor.

There are things you can do: Lose the weight! Stop biting your nails! Whiten your teeth! Look your best to attract the best potential life partners. I know that we don't like to think of this as a competition— but it is. You are competing with other women on campus for the attention of the best men. Give yourself every advantage.

It would be a shame to reach your thirties—single not by choice—and regret that you didn't put your best self forward when it would have done you the most good. You wore braces to straighten your teeth before adulthood—align the other elements of your physical appearance early so you approach your college years in peak form.

How you present yourself in your late teens and early twenties can set you up for a lifetime of happiness, or can hinder your ability to achieve all that you want for yourself. If you've struggled with obesity through most of your teen years, then maybe surgical intervention is a good idea for you. Remember that it's expensive, it hurts, and all surgery has some risks. But if cosmetic surgery can eradicate a haunting physical flaw and empower you with newfound confidence, then it's probably well worth the risks.

If you're going to go the route of cosmetic surgery, do it early enough to feel comfortable in your new body before going away to school. Don't wait until your thirties to get in your best shape. At that age, the number of your potential partners will be dramatically diminished, as will be your body's ability to rebound after surgery. You need to prepare yourself sooner than you think to make the best use of your college years and to ensure your personal happiness if that includes marriage and family.

I know women on campuses today with beautiful faces, gorgeous hair, and spectacular minds—but they are significantly overweight. They are seen as fat girls. I'm sure that they see themselves as fat girls. And this is such a sensitive issue that even I (who can almost always share candid advice) cannot bring myself to tell these girls directly what they need to hear: Eat less. Move more. I'm sure that there are multiple factors that contribute to a person's obesity—psychological, metabolic, genetic—but the fact is that you don't need to join an expensive gym or a commercial weight-loss program. Eat less. Move more.

And while we're talking personal . . . resist the temptation to wear the latest fashion if it just doesn't suit you. If you have short, stubby legs, a very short skirt is probably not a good look for you. Nor is a deeply plunging neckline especially flattering on most bodies—and it is especially unflattering in the message it sends to young men. Yes, you want men to look at you, but encourage them to look deeply into your eyes and not your cleavage. When my sons were of bar mitzvah age, it made me crazy to see twelve- and thirteen-year-old girls wearing backless, strapless dresses and high heels to the celebrations. Beyond being inappropriate attire for a house of worship, it is just wrong for little girls to be showing this amount of skin.

Equally cringe-worthy are mature women who insist on dressing like teenage girls. At twenty years old, you are at your most beautiful—your body is mature, but hasn't yet been altered by childbirth and the natural aging process. Dress beautifully. The torn blue jeans were okay in high school (not really), but you should look better than that in college.

Think about dressing prettily and age-appropriately for you.

Easier and faster than improving the shape of your body is beautifying the appearance of your hands. I have a particular bugaboo about nail biting. It is an especially unattractive habit. For me, a person with her fingers in her mouth looks exceedingly stupid. And it just isn't healthy to have fingers in your mouth. You know where they've been! Everywhere! And, stubby, chewed-up fingertips are ugly. A woman's hands should be graceful and beautiful. Care for your hands and manicure your nails. I was a nail biter all through high school. I know, it's a very difficult habit to break, because unlike smoking—where you don't have cigarettes to smoke if you don't buy them—your nails are always with you. But I always envied girls with beautiful nails and resolved the summer before I went away to college that I would quit biting my nails. It takes only a couple of weeks for bitten nails to grow out, and beautifully manicured nails look great. There really are no tricks to stop nail biting. You have to keep those fingers out of your mouth!

It is hard to break bad habits. Just do it. Commit yourself to doing what you know is good for you.

Do everything you can to look your very best. You'll be a man magnet. But what's more important, you'll feel better about yourself, you'll be healthier, and you'll be more confident.

Smart Advice

- Prepare yourself to be as socially successful in college as possible. If you require major bodywork, get it done in high school.
- Dress like the beautiful woman you are.
- Beautiful is as beautiful does. Be nice!

Be a Better Girlfriend

*D*ATING IS HARD FOR EVERYONE, BECAUSE WHOM WE DATE IS A DEC-laration of self-worth. The comment "He/she's out of your league" recognizes that we are generally best served by dating people who are at our level. Many things define that level, including good looks, social status, intellect, and wealth, to name a few. For a *six* to date a *ten* is asking for trouble. It's unbalanced. The ten is probably thinking that they can do better, and the six will never feel secure in the relationship. The truth is that the ten *can* do better, and the six knows that. All measures need not be equal, but the sum total needs to be pretty close in order for a partnership to be on good footing. Who we date says a lot about who we think we are.

The interesting thing is that sometimes we misevaluate potential partners. Don't be so quick to dismiss a possibly great date for unimportant reasons. He might be better than you give him credit for. No, he's probably not perfect, but neither are you. Think about whether it might be a good idea to make allowances for his shyness, awkwardness, sloppy clothes, and unexplainable enthusiasm for Neil Diamond. And entering into a relationship with the idea that you can *fix him* is a mistake; maybe the fault, dear Brutus, is not in your date, but in yourself.

When I was a freshman, Princeton was barely coeducational. There were only two hundred women in my class of almost one thousand students. We were not especially nice to the men on campus. There were so few of us and so many of them that we could afford to be a bit haughty—or, so we thought. In truth, the men weren't always kind to us, either. Many were still in the habit of busing in women for the weekend. For more than two hundred years the university had only male students, so the tradition of importing girls on Friday night was firmly entrenched in campus culture. Old habits die hard. In thinking back over those early days of coeducation, we should have been kinder to our male classmates back then, and you should be kinder to your male classmates now.

Remember those quiet, shy guys I told you to look for? Those guys would probably also be very good boyfriends, if they were with women who were good girlfriends. They might be inexperienced and insecure, and when people are unsure of themselves, they act oddly. If women treat them with kindness and respect, they'll feel secure—and everyone is more enjoyable to be with when they aren't nervous. In every circumstance, personal or professional, if you act in a manner that encourages others to feel good about themselves, they will feel good about you.

Tormenting suitors by putting them down or talking about old boyfriends is a game that women have played for a very long time. It's rude and unkind, and there are better ways of attracting and keeping a man's attention. Dating isn't a predatory sport; neither party needs to *win* or sacrifice the other to claim victory. By our actions, we provide a road map for how we expect to be treated by others. Be nice, sweet, kind, loyal, supportive, and most of all, be fun. The best partnerships and marriages are distinguished by the ability to laugh together. The inevitable vicissitudes of life offer enough to cry over; neither your date nor your spouse should add to that strife. Instead, they should be a reliable source of support and good humor in trying times. Kindness inspires kindness, generosity inspires generosity, and getting to know each other through dating can be . . . fun!

Fun on a date doesn't begin in bed. Depending on the kind of relationship you are in, perhaps it ends there, but it definitely doesn't begin there. It sounds so old-fashioned (even to *my* ears) to suggest that you *save some magic for the honeymoon*, but it's actually pretty good advice. If you start in the bedroom, where is there to go? And it would be a shame to miss the joy of courtship. It's romantic and it's how young people get to know each other. Even young men who are ever eager to have sex know that it is a wise and special woman who takes it slow, and allows a friendship to grow before things get too serious. Relationships take time to develop, and the slow dance toward intimacy is so joyous that you won't want to sit that one out.

Good male friends often make good boyfriends. If you get along with him, you might want to consider him as a potential mate—even if he's not the hottest guy in the room.

In early adulthood, we try out different personae as we strive to understand our authentic selves. When we date, it's as if the stage is set for the audition of these different personality types. Think carefully about whom you model yourself after, because that's how your date—and the world will see you. And it is how you will come to see yourself. Who you are as a girlfriend is a harbinger of who you will be as a wife. Consider comporting yourself with the dignity, grace, and elegance of Audrey Hepburn, Grace Kelly, or Jacqueline Kennedy Onassis. These were women of outstanding character, beloved by all and desired by men of substance. Resist the temptation to go the route of the seductress or the spitfire. Women who exude nothing but sexuality grow tiresome quickly, and relationships that are based only on physical connection have little chance of surviving.

The sassy bad girl might seem like fun, but even Rhett Butler, the ultimate bad boy, could take only so much of Scarlett O'Hara's spunk and selfishness before, frankly, my dear, he just didn't give a damn.

Smart Advice

- Look past his superficial flaws; he might be a diamond in the rough.
- Your kindness and respect can bring out the best in him.
- Serious romance starts with friendship and a well-paced courtship.

Be a Better Girlfriend . . .
to Your Girlfriends

*Y*OU NEED LOTS OF DIFFERENT TYPES OF FRIENDS. THEY SATISFY A variety of appetites the way a banquet satisfies different tastes on your palate. Your best friends don't need to think the way you do, but you have to believe they come by their opinions honestly and that they are truthful in their dealings with you. There is little that is more satisfying or more valuable than the exchange of ideas among intelligent people who disagree.

Sometimes it's hard to recognize your best friends when you first meet them. They may not look or sound like what you expect. I met my best friend in my freshman year at Princeton. At first, I did not like her . . . at all. She liked me even less. She was (and still is) a thin, gorgeous blonde descended from a *Mayflower* family, an Episcopalian who went to private school in Westport, Connecticut, had relatives who sailed on the *Titanic*, and grew up in a two-hundred-year-old home filled with heirlooms. There just didn't seem to be a lot there to which I could relate. All of my relatives perished in World War II, so far from having a well-articulated family tree, my parents were like Adam and

Eve. I'm Jewish, went to New York City public schools, and lived in the Bronx. What's not to like about that?

By the time we met in college, I had never been to a cocktail party, didn't own a black dress, and was quite lacking the social graces that were second nature to my best friend. But we bonded over a language disagreement in the basement of McCarter Theatre one evening. Forty years later, we still almost never agree. But I trust her always and that's all that matters.

College is a wonderful place to find your lifelong friends. You've reached adulthood, and the amazing experiences you share during your undergraduate years will stay with you forever, and remain joyous memories when you can recollect them with the people who knew you when. Look for classmates whom you admire and can learn from. Seek out the ones who make you laugh—they are easy to be with and giggling is good for your soul. Find others who make you think—they are *not* as easy to be with, but because they are challenging, being with them forces you to dig deeper into who you are and what you know. You'll need some sensitive friends, ones who are good communicators and will comfort you in trying times. Competitive friends (if they're not ugly about competition) can inspire you to rise above your complacency. Be open-minded and develop a broad spectrum of cohorts and colleagues.

You may even have an *imaginary* friend. You know, a real person whom you've felt close to your whole life but have never met. For me, that's Caroline Kennedy. I know this might seem like a million years ago, but I grew up around the same time that Caroline Kennedy was growing up. I used to wish I had her perfect blond hair, her very American parents, and her pony named Macaroni, if you can believe it. I had curly black hair, very European parents, and a canary who had no name, if you can believe that too. Her father was the president of the United

States and my pop worked in a grocery store. She had grandparents, and I had none; we both had a brother. When I went to Princeton, she went to Harvard (which is a good school too).

We both married Jewish men in 1986, had our first baby in 1988, and had our last baby four years later. We both live on the Upper East Side. In 1993, our baby boys each had the same blue Maclaren stroller. I know this because one morning I was pushing my baby in his stroller up York Avenue after dropping his older brother off at elementary school. We pushed to the top of the hill on Eighty-Third Street to wait for the light to change and there was Caroline and her baby, little John Kennedy Schlossberg, in the same stroller waiting for the same light to change.

I greeted her with the big hello that is reserved for people whom I just love but haven't seen in much too long. I've felt so close to her for so many decades that I forgot that we'd never actually met.

She was absolutely lovely—surprised at how enthusiastically I greeted her but genuinely gracious. We chatted about the babies for a few minutes, and then she went east across Eighty-Third and I continued north to Eighty-Sixth Street.

I've always admired Caroline. Although we haven't met again since that day at the street corner, she continues to be an inspiration to me and I think of her as a *special* kind of friend . . . the kind who doesn't ask for any of my time, or for favors, or for patience or a sympathetic ear, but serves as a measure of what women of our vintage are capable of achieving and overcoming.

Friendships are like insurance policies and need to be examined periodically to ensure that they continue meet your needs. You have to be aware of the friends who have become toxic and cut them loose before they become a major drain on your time, energy, and confidence.

Having a good friend requires being a good friend. It's a relationship that is often out of balance, with one needing the immediate attention of the other, but is sustained by the promise of eventual equalization. The best friendships are rooted in a tacit understanding that you'll be there for each other in good times and bad. Both can be trying. Comforting a friend in the throes of divorce, or over the loss of a parent, a job, or (God forbid) a dog requires selflessness, especially if your friend is especially lugubrious. But you show up for your besties. Perhaps the greater test of friendship is the ability to be genuinely happy for your friend when they are blessed with extraordinary good fortune—especially if you have not been equally blessed. Hold a good thought that karma will eventually smile upon you—and know that your best friends will smile with you when that happens.

Invest in your relationships honestly, and recognize that at the heart of the best friendships is the truth.

Smart Advice

- Develop many different types of friendships because they support and delight you in different ways.
- College is the best time to find your lifelong friends, as a young adult with a long life ahead of you.
- The value of any friendship is measured by the commitment of both parties. Usually, you get as good as you give.
- Expect your friendships to change over time, just as you do.

PART II

Your Twenties

Okay, so you didn't find him on campus . . . now what? Focus! You're not getting any younger! The first ten years after college are absolutely critical for putting in place the components of your personal happiness. Of course, you want to launch your career, but if you aspire to marriage and motherhood the clock is ticking . . . loudly. Career goals can be delayed, but your prime fertility years are distinctly limited and can dissipate before your eyes.

Don't squander these most important years on men who aren't right for you, or in pursuing professional opportunities that can wait.

If you dream of a traditional family, your efforts and energies should be laser focused on finding a husband.

Here's how to date smarter now that you're in your twenties.

Things Your Twenty-Year-Old Self Can't Imagine

$\mathscr{A}$T TWENTY YEARS OLD, YOU CAN'T IMAGINE THAT YOU WILL EVER BE thirty-five, much less how quickly you'll get there. Young women don't seem cognizant of how fast we age, or even what different ages look like.

Your twenty-year-old self can't imagine that you will ever be too old for some men to even *consider* dating, or that when you are ready to finally settle down you won't find an eligible man who is appropriate for you, or that there will ever come a time that your eggs are no longer viable. Without getting into a discussion of the relative morality of premarital sex, the overriding concern of sexually active women during their college years is for *not* getting pregnant. I know that it's hard to imagine the sound of a ticking biological clock or that you might *ever* have difficulty conceiving a child, but fertility clinics and the offices of reproductive endocrinologists are filled with anxious and heartbroken women. There is simply nothing that will fill the hole in the heart of a woman who has to come to terms with the fact that she will never bear the children that she has dreamed of.

By the time you are in college, you start to become aware of the things that you know—and the things that you don't know. But the much larger segment of that pie chart is reserved for the things that you *don't even know* that you don't know! And I know that you don't know that. When a close friend's young son was approaching his sixth birthday, she asked him what sort of present he was hoping for to celebrate his special day. Imagine how stunned she was when he told her that he wanted "a Maxi Pad with Wings!" She asked him what exactly that was, and he told her, "It's a giant, soft thing that flies!" He went on to say, "And the ladies are all really happy to have them, Mommy!" Of course, the advertising of feminine hygiene products is so obtuse that it leaves a six-year-old completely baffled as to the purpose of these products. But he thought he got it right, and had no reason to believe that it was anything different than what he thought. Her son couldn't have known what he obviously didn't know—and neither can you.

You don't know how fast the fifteen years from twenty to thirty-five will pass. But it is critical that you clearly envision your thirty-five-year-old self in your late teens and early twenties and earnestly plan for the personal happiness you hope to achieve by that age. It will be upon you faster than you could ever imagine.

Be purposeful in how you spend these years, especially in terms of the men you date while you are a student.

Remember that you have a limited window of opportunity within which to bear your own children, and finding the right husband will be the cornerstone of your future happiness and the foundation of your future family.

Be methodical in how you choose your dates.

Don't waste your time or yourself on men who aren't appropriate for you. Look carefully at the men with whom you go to school. You will *never* again have this concentration of men who are worthy of you.

Another thing that your twenty-year-old self can't imagine is that even the geekiest guy on campus today will probably grow into the most amazing, accomplished man. Exactly the kind of man to whom you're going to want to be married! I remain very connected to my classmates and Princeton University because I serve as president of my class. And now, when I'm at alumni events with the men I knew as undergraduates, I marvel at who I thought they were back when we were students, and at the amazing men they have become today. Honestly, I didn't have the wisdom or the vision to see past their bell-bottom trousers, scraggly beards, stringy hair, or that disco look made so popular by John Travolta in *Saturday Night Fever*. The 1970s was a seriously unattractive decade, and very few people can pull off that black shirt/white suit look with any aplomb.

As a student, I was shortsighted, and I regret it. So many of the men whom I was very quick to dismiss then, I would be delighted to be with now. They are smart, accomplished, and gracious. We share the very extraordinary experience of our undergraduate years, and none of them wear bell-bottoms any more! Almost uniformly, they have aged beautifully. Many have less hair and larger waistlines, but they are all well groomed and look wonderful in smartly tailored suits.

When you consider the men in your class, I urge you to look past their sloppy clothes, their awkwardness, their immaturity, and try to imagine who and what they will become. Trust me . . . just as you are, they are destined for greatness.

Of course, not every one of your male classmates is a winner. For decades after graduation, I thought about one classmate whom I was sweet on all through our undergraduate years. We were friends and when we were twenty years old, I thought we were well suited to be more than that. He didn't think so. It wasn't until very recently that my regrets were recalibrated by other classmates who told me how badly he has always treated the women he was with.

It's funny that sometimes the one that got away—was actually the bullet you narrowly escaped.

Smart Advice

- The fifteen years from twenty to thirty-five go much faster than you think.
- Be methodical in how you choose your dates as a student. The twenty-year-old geek could grow into an amazingly successful forty-year-old stud!
- Look carefully at the men with whom you go to school. You will *never* again have this concentration of amazing men to choose from.

Husband Hunting in the Real World

$\mathcal{Y}$OU'RE IN YOUR TWENTIES, YOU'RE NO LONGER A STUDENT, AND YOU are hoping to find a husband in a nonacademic setting. Good luck! You'll need it.

Despite the concentration of age-appropriate, single, like-minded men on campus, not all women are fortunate enough to meet their match while they are still students. Can you find great men after you graduate? Of course—you just won't find as many of them in one place as you found when you were in school. And the nature of being in classes and extracurricular activities with your peers was an *organic* way to get to know people and determine whether there was attraction enough to explore pursuing a relationship. But now, beyond being an inelegant path to romance, nightclubs and online dating plunk you face-to-face with people who are there as you are . . . hunting for a mate. It can often seem desperate, unnatural, and almost predatory to judge and be judged in such a blatant way.

So, where can you meet someone after you graduate? At work? Many people do, but it's a bad idea to get romantically involved with someone you work with—and some companies even prohibit or regulate it. I understand that most people spend *so* much time at work, there almost isn't any time outside the office. And working together professionally is in some ways not unlike working together as students. You are in each other's company for extended periods of time, engaged in shared corporate or professional activities, and have the ability to evaluate your coworkers in a nonpressured environment.

You're not at work to find a husband, just like you were not at school to get that MRS degree. But because that *isn't* the main reason you're there (unlike Match.com or JDate), it allows you to get to know and evaluate your colleagues organically. It's natural that attractions will form and flirtations will begin, but know that the office romance is fraught with hazard—especially for women.

I suppose it sometimes happens that a male executive assistant falls for the woman who manages the department, but the much more common scenario is the younger, less experienced woman becoming involved with an older man with seniority. While a torrid love affair with your boss can feel very romantic and sophisticated, if and when it ends (and it almost always ends) both of you will find working in the same office to be uncomfortable—if not unbearable.

And if it is impossible to continue to work together, which of the two of you is going to be forced to resign? You seriously put your career at risk with romantic entanglements on the job. As a seasoned HR babe, I'm telling you that if you hope to advance in your company and your industry, don't *dip your pen in the company ink*, and don't develop a reputation for trying to advance yourself professionally by making yourself available personally. It just isn't worth it.

In the 1970s and 1980s, New York City had a proliferation of singles bars where hopeful twenty- or thirty-somethings would go to find love. I am told that it was an appalling scene. The men were frequently older and sometimes married. The women would often get tarted up beyond reason to attract the attention of available men. Deceit and desperation filled the air. Ugh. It was a demeaning and sometimes dangerous way for young women to meet men. The clubs that are today's equivalent of those singles bars offer similar atmospheres and pose similar risks to women who don't know anything about the men they are meeting—other than that they want a woman. Online dating can be the equivalent of going to a singles bar . . . for lazy people. It's the same brazen hunt for love or sex, from the convenience of your own home! Yes, I know that many people meet online and sometimes it works out well, but it is frequently inelegant, undignified, and hazardous—and you'll find even more of those married men trolling for single women.

So, where should you be looking to find a life partner? I'd love to think that you will meet someone at your synagogue, church, temple, or mosque. Clearly, the people there share your religious beliefs and anyone who attends services regularly is probably living a relatively decent and upstanding life.

But how many of your friends regularly visit a house of worship? I know, not too many. Think about it. It is a safe and reasonable place to meet people who probably share at least some of your values, and your clergy can probably introduce you to the members of your congregation who are also single. In fact, I bet that they'd be delighted to do so.

Blind dates presumably have the benefit of personal recommendation from the person who thought to connect the two of you. They will know if he is actually married, and can assure him that the photo he's seen of you is relatively recent. And there is the element of responsibility that both parties share for being gracious, because you can and probably *will* both report back to the arranger of the blind date. This accountability keeps everyone honest.

Unfortunately, this kind of fix-up seems to be waning in popularity. While some friends are happy to act as matchmaker, when things don't work out—or end badly—they risk losing *two* friends. So figure out who are the people in your life you trust, people you can tell would be receptive to introducing you to single men who may be appropriate for you. They may not know anyone or be comfortable making such introductions—but it doesn't hurt to ask. And they *may* know someone but have been reluctant to suggest a meeting for fear of seeming meddlesome or presumptuous.

And stay connected with your school. Your college years were clearly the best time and place to meet and get to know men in a comfortable, safe, and informal environment, but if you didn't find your life partner on campus, get involved with alumni activities. Get involved in alumni affairs, attend your class reunions, and participate in programs and workshops that are sponsored by regional or local groups associated with your school. You might learn something, and you might meet someone who also has a passion for continuing education.

Smart Advice

- Office romance is fraught with hazard, especially for women. Look elsewhere.

- Look for men in settings that are more organic than online or in singles bars.

- Remain connected with your school and classmates through alumni activities.

- Tell people whom you know and trust that you would be receptive to an introduction. You never know.

What the Feminist Movement Did . . . and What It Didn't Do

I AM FREQUENTLY ASKED IF I AM A FEMINIST. HONESTLY, I'M NOT even sure I know what a feminist is anymore.

When the pioneer feminists gathered for the first women's rights convention in Seneca Falls, New York, in 1848, their Declaration of Sentiments was intended to achieve civil, social, political, and religious rights for women. All women owe a debt of gratitude to these heroines for our ability to vote, own property, sign contracts, and for many other things that today we take for granted.

Like most groups, women have always needed and still do need advocacy groups to ensure that their rights are protected. But I'd bet that Elizabeth Cady Stanton never could have imagined how the noble mission of these brave suffragettes would be subverted over 150 years to include the emasculation of men, the elimination of romantic courtship, and the conclusion that marriage and motherhood are primary obstacles to the empowerment of women.

This is the unfortunate result of modern feminists who have crossed over to the dark side.

The feminist movement advanced women beyond a place where they had to passively settle for homemaking to the exclusion of all other aspirations. Clearly I was an early beneficiary of the admirable accomplishments of the feminist movement in the 1960s and 1970s. Princeton and other Ivy League universities probably would have remained all male if pressure from the women's movement hadn't demanded a serious reevaluation of, among other things, two-hundred-year-old university policies, which led to the adoption of coeducation.

Unfortunately, extreme feminist doctrine has left those who *do* dream of blissful domesticity feeling dismissed and disrespected and sometimes looked down upon as betrayers to the sisterhood. This is *not* what the women's movement was supposed to do. The goal of empowering *all* women is inconsistent with the bullying of those women who aspire to more conservative, traditional roles.

When I was a college student, feminists were tough girls who didn't wear makeup or bras. To me, it seemed that they tried to act like men and look like men. Being a poor girl from the Bronx, perhaps my ability to discern the difference between feminists and lesbians was limited. It still is. I used to think a feminist was a person who believed that women should be afforded the same rights and opportunities as men. This includes equal pay for equal work, and the ability to choose not to get pregnant through the use of contraceptives. But it's difficult to take seriously women's rights advocates who intimidate young women who want traditional marriage and family.

Men aren't the enemy. The aggressive and relentless feminist message of male uselessness is both ridiculous and counterproductive. Women who aspire to bear their own children in a traditional marriage most certainly need men.

This predatory approach of women's rights at the expense of male acceptance hasn't helped women and has been socially destructive on many levels. Masculinity is not oppressive and chivalry is not inappropriate. The radical feminists' contempt for marriage has left many women trying to construct a family life from the ashes of the cherished institution that the women's movement has tried to burn to the ground. This hasn't helped women.

The banner of feminism began to fray when instead of focusing on gaining respect for women and the choices they may want to make, it tried to force the unreasonable notion that men and women were not different in any substantial way. That is nonsense. Men and women are most certainly different in many and important ways. The core principle of the movement was for women to gain respect *as* women, and to empower them to do all that they want to do. It was not to respect women because they're *just like men.* There are distinct gender differences, and the feminist mantra of "I can do it myself" is shortsighted. Independence is admirable, but children need a father. Beyond the obvious necessity for male genetic material in the conception of children, why would a woman want to go through life alone?

So what did the feminist movement actually achieve? Equal pay? Nope. Women still earn significantly less than men doing like work. The Equal Rights Amendment has not passed—and many feel that it is unnecessary legislation seeking redundant equalities. In shunning notions of sexual propriety as antiquated, the women's movement has given license to sexual freedom for women. The unfortunate by-product of this freedom is the idea that marriage is something women might hope for *after* having sex. This puts inordinate pressure on them to be sexually attractive and sexually competitive. Again, think about cows and free milk.

Of course, women are no longer treated as property. We vote, we run for political office, we run businesses. We dream bigger dreams than our mothers or grandmothers could ever have imagined. Most women view education not just as "something to fall back on," but as prerequisite to a fulfilling career. For these things and more, the women's movement should be credited.

Needless to say, women in almost every profession once available only to men owe a debt of gratitude to the pioneer women who forged these paths. That should have been the legacy of the women's movement—but they went too far, and that confuses me.

For the most part, these were smart women. They must have known that their anti-male rhetoric and unattractive behavior would result in a backlash. They might not have called it hubris, but it was. The arrogance of the most vocal and extreme feminist proponents has hurt more women than it has helped, and resulted in a reversal of some of the gains that were made.

Of course, they will blame these setbacks on male testosterone and misogyny—but that's what hubris is.

Smart Advice

- Reject feminist doctrine that dismisses and disrespects women who embrace traditional roles of wife and mother.
- Feminism was supposed to empower women to pursue *all* that they want for themselves—even that which is politically incorrect.
- Men aren't the enemy. Men are wonderful!

Stupid Juice

*I*F YOU ASSOCIATE TOO CLOSELY WITH A MAN WHO IS SIGNIFICANTLY below your intellectual level, you will eventually get *stupid juice* all over you.

Trust me . . . no amount of Clorox will ever get *that* stain all out.

THERE ARE THINGS WE SURMISE about others based upon the people with whom they associate. And while it is human nature to gravitate toward those we look up to and hope to learn from, it's reasonable to assume that the intimate circle of friends we keep (and certainly our choice of spouse) reflects a lot about who we are. We reassure others of our worth and character when we hitch our wagon to admirable stars that reflect well on us. And there is *self*-affirmation that comes from associating with people whom we respect and admire. It is not uncommon in our adult lives to sometimes feel disenfranchised by a group of friends that no longer suit us, or who have grown in directions that are inconsistent with our own growth. We are defined, and we define ourselves, by the company we keep.

Of course, there are many things that define you: your family, personal history, academic credentials, professional persona, accomplishments and failures, attitudes and perspectives, and dozens of other identifying markers. If you marry, there is nothing that will define you more clearly or have a greater impact on your future success than your choice of spouse.

Oddly, some people take great umbrage at the suggestion that as a woman, you are defined by your husband. However, in many and *important* ways you most certainly are. Think about the official and commercial institutions that will provide or deny you services based upon who your husband is: the federal government, banks and mortgage lenders, the IRS, insurance companies, and health-care providers, to name a few.

This is not to say that because a woman is defined by her spouse in some ways, that her own identity is subsumed by her husband, or that single women are lacking *any* identity. Or that to validate womanhood requires a husband. None of these erroneous assumptions has anything to do with the practical realities of how your spouse's credentials will impact your options and opportunities.

Your friends and family may not judge you by the man you marry, but chances are, yeah . . . they will. And why wouldn't they? Who you choose to marry says a lot about you. You don't choose your parents or your children, but you do choose your spouse, and your choice is an undeniable statement of whom you see yourself as, and how you see your place in the world. Certainly, women marry for different reasons. There are the dreamers, the pragmatists, the gold diggers, and the social climbers, to name a few. Some women marry multiple times for different reasons. Jacqueline Kennedy Onassis famously said that the first time you marry for love, the second for money, and the third for companionship. That's probably true. In every stage of a woman's life, she defines her own need for a man differently.

Classic literature speaks to the stages of womanhood as maiden, mother, and crone. Very young women are romantics and hear love songs on windswept beaches, where they hold hands with athletic men whose children they hope to someday bear. A middle-aged woman has transitioned past the wide-eyed innocence and knows the importance of security and the value of a man who can provide for her and their family. Older women have been there and done that. They are grateful for having lived as long as they have and just don't want to be alone. Or, in the words of Stephen Sondheim, "First you're another sloe-eyed vamp, then someone's mother, then you're camp." In each of these stages, the man you're with defines the woman you are.

Here's the most important thing . . . you will come to define *yourself* by your spouse. If you marry a man who isn't worthy of you, it will eventually chip away at your self-esteem and you will start to believe that this is all *you* are worth. That's not to say that you can't be happy with the good-hearted plumber, but if your education and ambition can propel you to stratospheric success, it may not be easy to accept your status as the plumber's wife. And it may be difficult for you to be gracious about others introducing you as Mrs. Joe the Plumber.

Of course, you could recalibrate your expectations and embrace a lower socioeconomic level, but if you don't think that you could comfortably do so, you have to set your sights higher. This is your other half, the person you tell the world and yourself that you've chosen to share a life, share a bed, share a home, and raise a family.

I know that every Ivy League graduate isn't always brilliant, and some of the smartest people in the world are lacking formal education. I play a lot of online Scrabble. One of my favorite opponents is a seventy-year-old, Scottish, retired filling-station owner in Vancouver. I don't know where he went to school, but I don't think it was Cambridge or Oxford. My Princeton degree probably trumps his academic credentials, but I can't beat him in Scrabble.

Smart comes in many forms and is sometimes disguised behind very humble façades. Stupid is unmistakable.

"You are judged by the company you keep, so choose your friends wisely." My mother used to say that. And it's true.

Intelligence is a reasonable predictor of many qualities that you will want in your mate. Remember that your husband's stability, creditworthiness, and character will factor heavily into many decisions that you will want to go your way. And even without procreation, the right husband will help you define the trajectory of your life, applaud and encourage your capacity for greatness, and make your victories more joyous just by sharing them.

Smart Advice

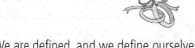

- We are defined, and we define ourselves, by the company we keep. In large part, the man you're with defines the woman you are.
- Your spouse's credentials will impact your options and opportunities.
- If you marry a man who isn't worthy of you, it will eventually chip away at your self-esteem.
- *Smart* is sometimes disguised. Stupid is unmistakable.

Go for the Best Credentials

*T*HE UNIVERSE OF POSSIBLE HUSBANDS IS SO VAST, HOW DO YOU EVEN begin to separate the wheat from the chaff? The same way that you filter your options in every other aspect of your life—by examining past performance and credentials. Understanding the true benefit of every possible employer or institution of higher education would be unreasonably time consuming and labor intensive. Instinctively, we pare down the potential options to a manageable number by filtering for certain criteria. A long-established business with a track record of success and innovation is well worth interviewing with. If academic distinction is at the top of your list in choosing a college, schools that have produced multiple Rhodes scholars should be considered. Similarly, you can sharpen your search for a potential husband through filters that examine credentials—personal, professional, and academic.

Your credentials enter the room before you do. They are the banner that announces who you are, until time, circumstance, and experience allow you to demonstrate your actual qualifications, competencies, and authority.

When you are choosing a school, a job, or a life partner, credentials are important. The reputation and track record of a man, an academic institution, or a business should be a *significant* consideration when choosing among many options. Resist the temptation to go to that quaint, little-known college in one of those square midwestern states. No one has ever heard of it, and your diploma from the College of Nowhere will necessitate your spending the first several minutes of any job interview trying to explain where you went to school—if you're even able to score a meeting with those credentials. What you majored in doesn't matter, but the reputation of your school assures possible employers that you are a candidate worth considering. A degree in advanced biomedical engineering and experimental physics from Podunk University can't compare to an A.B. in English from Yale. No, Podunk U doesn't actually offer a degree in advanced biomedical engineering and experimental physics. And there is no university in Podunk. In fact, there is no Podunk anywhere worthy of a convenience store, never mind a university. But you get my point.

If as a high school senior you are admitted to many excellent colleges, choose the one that's closest to the top of the list of "best schools." You probably have an equal chance of being happy at almost any school, so opt for the most impressive credential. It will stand you in good stead for a lifetime. I understand that not everyone gets into Princeton. I frequently say that to people who went to Harvard. It makes their heads explode.

Likewise, if you are evaluating multiple job offers, choose the most recognizable and respected company. I regularly counsel candidates who are considering many job offers to opt for the company with the best reputation—assuming that the opportunity, compensation, and benefits are comparable—because *that* credential will be the most meaningful to future employers and afford candidates the best options moving forward.

When I was first starting my career after college, I worked for a small company that manufactured colored plastic lipstick tubes and fingernails matched to product for display purposes in the cosmetic industry. It was a family-owned business and produced a fairly esoteric product. In social settings, I was always struggling to find an easy way of explaining what I did and the company I did it for. It usually took a lot of words and most of the time people would nod and smile without really understanding. A few years later I went to work for Citibank. Wow . . . what a difference. "Susan, what do you do?" "I work for Citibank." Boom. No explanation needed. Instead of a big job in a small start-up, you are better off opting for a smaller job in a much bigger, more recognizable company.

In choosing a husband, how important are credentials? Extremely important.

Is every man who went to Princeton, Harvard, or Yale a good catch? No, of course not.

But a luxurious academic credential is a very good indicator of a man's ambition, his record of academic achievement, and, very likely, his future success.

Is working for Google, American Express, or Goldman Sachs a guarantee that a man will always do well and be able to support a family? Obviously not. There are exceptions to every rule, but these outstanding companies are extremely selective in whom they hire. They have a reputation for excellence to protect and they look for candidates from the best colleges and the best companies for the same reason that you should. Credentials matter. As a human resources consultant, I know that sometimes a hiring manager will opt for a slightly less qualified candidate from a more impressive school or company as a CYA (cover your ass) measure. In the event the hire doesn't work out, they can justify their choice to their own management by saying something like "The guy went to Dartmouth and worked for Deloitte." A poor hiring decision isn't easily forgiven if the guy went to Podunk University and worked for IpsyPipsy.com.

Of course, credentials aren't the only criteria you should consider, but they are a reasonably good predictor of what you can expect in a husband, school, or job. Especially when evaluating a potential spouse, there are numerous intangible factors to be considered, and the qualities that arouse interest in the opposite sex are different for everyone.

Obviously, there are no guarantees that the best credentials will make you happy, but in the absence of other data, they are a very reasonable measure and indicator of quality. Whom you are married to, where you went to school, and where you've worked are touchstone components of your personal architecture . . . forever. Long before people get to know you, they will probably be aware of these elements of your history.

Make choices that represent you well, that you will be proud of, and that will require neither explanation nor apology.

Smart Advice

- Credentials matter. They are what people know about you before they know you.
- Life changes, but credentials are etched in stone.
- The quality of a man's education and the company he works for are good indications of his ambition and future success. Go for the best!

Birds of a Feather

$\mathcal{M}$ARRYING SOMEONE OF YOUR OWN RACE AND RELIGION IS easier—unless, of course, you happen to fall in love with someone who is neither.

Serious relationships and marriage are challenging in so many ways and for so many reasons. Putting someone else's needs before your own, accepting the quirks and peculiarities of another, considering how what you do and say will impact your partner . . . these can all get in the way of a joyous union. The added complications of different cultural orientation or the disapproval of others can be destructive to a relationship. It is sometimes suggested to young women that it is "just as easy to fall in love with a rich man as it is with a poor man." The biggest reason to hope that you fall in love with someone of your same race and religion is that it's just easier.

I know many interfaith couples as well as a few interracial pairings. Some are very happy unions and others are not, just the same as single-religion and single-race relationships can be. I can't say for sure that the religious or racial differences account for the unhappiness in those couples, but it undeniably adds to the pressures on them. These couples can arrange it so that their daily lives are not profoundly affected by their differences, but milestone events and holidays can be very problematic for mixed marriages and families.

Even if you are not observant, your religion probably occupies a place in your heart and mind. Maybe it's a nostalgic place that reminds you of your childhood and your family. Whether you spin dreidels at Hanukkah or sing carols at Christmas, these are the rituals that stay with you and that you'll probably want to share with your own children. It is absolutely soul satisfying to introduce new generations to the cherished traditions that you grew up with.

In mixed-background marriages, the questions of which traditions are celebrated—and when—can create stress.

We can embrace each other's religious observances as long as they don't require our sacrificing our own. Especially when it comes to children. You might not have a big problem being married by a priest instead of a rabbi, or baking a ham for Easter instead of braising a brisket for Rosh Hashanah, but when it comes to our children's fulfilling sacred commandments, even the most unreligious of us can become very territorial. This is why finding someone who was brought up as you were, and with the same expectations and respect for the same religious traditions, can be helpful. If you're Jewish you won't want to argue with your non-Jewish spouse about whether your son will be circumcised, or whether your children will attend Hebrew school to prepare for becoming a bar/bat mitzvah. If you're Christian, it's probably important to you to have your baby baptized, and to have your children attend Sunday school in preparation for confirmation. I hope you embrace your religion—any religion. Spiritual connectivity is comforting and helps remind you of your place in the world. It can also provide as much unexpected relief and feeling of cleanliness as a good sneeze. God bless you!

Of course, it can also be wonderful to introduce your religious customs to people of other faiths. My best friend is an Episcopalian. For almost forty years, we have celebrated each other's holidays together. Before her family started coming to my home for Passover seder, they didn't know what end of the matzo the balls came from. And there were things about Christmas that I didn't really understand either.

I'll always remember my first Christmas with her family in Westport . . . and you don't get more Christmassy than yuletide in Connecticut. On Christmas Eve, Kendall, her sister Cynthia, and I all slept in twin beds in the attic and the next morning awoke to stockings on the end of our beds. We all had many of the same things in our stockings, like an orange and a toothbrush, but we each had a couple of things that were unique. Kendall had a hairbrush, Cynthia had a set of magnets, and I had a bottle of plant food.

I couldn't understand why they gave me plant food.

I lived in a virtually windowless apartment in Manhattan with no plants. I didn't know what to think. We went downstairs to the living room with its beautifully decorated tree and mountains of gifts. I brought presents that I made for everyone, and there were many boxes for me. It was just perfect, like a Norman Rockwell magazine cover.

At the end of the weekend, I boarded the train back to the city still thinking about the plant food. I thought that maybe this is what gentiles do when Jewish girls join them for Christmas—give them plant food as a symbol of growth and fertility! Yes, that must be it.

It wasn't until many months later that I learned that Kendall's parents had bought me a hanging fern (for my sunless, plantless apartment) that they cleverly hid in their upstairs bathroom so I wouldn't see it before Christmas morning, and completely forgot about it until long after I had left to go home.

Every year we double over laughing as we retell the story of the "Christmas Miracle-Gro."

Everyone's spiritual identity is important, and it's easier for children to absorb a unified message of their religious and cultural background. It helps them know who they are in the world. Interfaith and interracial couples who can jointly communicate their own particular unified message can raise well-adjusted, engaged, and perfectly happy children. But other children grow up profoundly confused. Their disorientation is frequently fueled by the disgruntled in-laws who were never comfortable with the mixed marriage in the first place. If you're lucky, your parents and in-laws will keep their disapproval to themselves. But it's human nature for them to want you to raise your children exactly as they raised theirs, and there are probably many other ways in which they can hardly stand to see how you are bringing up their precious grandchildren.

And don't look to your spouse to intercede. In any fight between one's spouse and one's parents, no one wins.

The concept of "opposites attract" maybe works with electromagnetic theory—but this opposition may not work so well day after day in a lifelong relationship.

Life is filled with challenges and even the best marriages founded on core commonalities inevitably face difficulties.

Smart Advice

- Sharing religious traditions is wonderful, but mixed marriages require extra finesse to remain cohesive while respecting differing spiritual identities.

- Extended families aren't always accepting of a spouse who is different. Good luck with that.

- It's easier to sing out of the same hymnal if you share a similar background (have actually sung out of the same hymnal).

"He's Too Old for You!"
"She's Too Young for You!"

$\mathcal{I}$ WAS EIGHT YEARS OLD WHEN PRESIDENT KENNEDY WAS ASSASSI-
nated. My litmus test for whether a man is too young for me is whether
or not he remembers those bleak days of our childhood at the end of November 1963. Being sent home from school, the Zapruder film, Lee Har-
vey Oswald gunned down by Jack Ruby in the basement of the Dallas
police station, the riderless horse, little John John saluting his father's
casket, the grim funeral of our fallen president. If a man doesn't remember these transformative events that changed the world forever, he's too
young for me.

One thing I haven't exactly figured out, though, is how to gauge
if a man is too *old* for me. If he's no longer on solid food, that's a deal
breaker. If he can't walk without a walker and all of his college roommates are dead, he's probably out of my age group.

In our fifties, it's a little harder to determine if a date is too old for
us. Clearly, some people age better than others—so you can't always
judge by looks. Nor does age appropriateness matter as much when
you're older. But if you are a very young woman, I urge you to resist the

temptation to date much older men. When you are twenty-four years old, it may seem very romantic to date a man who is forty-five, but there is nothing romantic about being relegated to picking up his prescriptions and taking him to his doctor's appointments when he's almost seventy and you are still in your forties.

And then there is the issue of sex. Do you really want to have sex with a man old enough to be your father?

Of course, the May-December romance is nothing new. Beyond tabloid fodder of younger women with men who are considerable older, wealthier, and more socially prominent, many women seem to gravitate toward men who are more than a decade older than they are. In the case of Anna Nicole Smith's thirteen-month marriage to oil tycoon J. Howard Marshall II, who was sixty-three years her senior (she was twenty-six and he was eighty-nine), I think we can all agree on what Anna got out of that relationship.

I suppose that older men are attracted to very young women for the same reasons that younger men are attracted to them—they are beautiful. Men have always fantasized about being (aka "having sex") with young girls. The geezers have the additional impetus of trying to reaffirm their youth and virility by having a twenty-six-year-old knockout on their arm. If they are wealthy enough and generous enough to share their riches with willing young women, then it would seem all parties are well served. But why would a brilliant, well-educated young woman who is capable of building her own fortune choose to sacrifice her best years to elder caretaking?

And then, of course, there's the question of who will take care of you when *you're* that old.

Regardless of what you might stand to inherit, it's rarely a good enough trade-off. Your youth is fleeting. Try to share it with a man who is close to your same age, healthy, and vigorous. You'll take care of each other in your dotage.

As a Princetonian, I'd rather talk tigers than cougars, but the phenomenon of older women dating much younger men has become enough of a thing to merit a brief discussion. I suppose that it's only fair that as women become more successful and capable of "buying" a much younger companion, this curious trend will continue. Demi Moore is more than fifteen years older than Ashton Kutcher, (almost) old enough to be his mother. He broke up with her and began dating the much younger Mila Kunis. Maybe it's just a power thing for successful women, but I can't think of anything that makes a woman look older than being on the arm of a man who is easily mistaken as her son.

Appearances aside, being with a partner of your same vintage allows you both to share soft remembrances and subtle responses. When I find an American flag in a closet or a cabinet, I still count the stars. It goes back to my years in elementary school in the early 1960s when the U.S. flag changed from having forty-nine stars to having fifty. When we looked for a flag to hang in our classroom, we would first count the stars to make sure we had the right flag. Old habits die hard.

Having lived through the assassinations of President Kennedy, Robert Kennedy, and Martin Luther King, my heart still stops when regular television programming is interrupted by a "special report." Even though most of these broadcasts are now political news, weather warnings, and other noteworthy but not earth-shattering events, I stop what I am doing and am transfixed until reassurance comes that nobody has been assassinated. People who didn't grow up when I grew up probably can't begin to understand why anyone would count stars on an American flag or why the thumping sound that cuts into daytime viewing and heralds breaking news is still terrifying to me. These are the small things that unite a specific age group. I'm sure every age has its own seemingly insignificant markers that connect us to our peers.

Find someone your own age. Be young together. Grow old together.

Smart Advice

- Find someone your own age.
- Be young together.
- Grow old together.

Mr. Right?

*H*OW DO YOU KNOW IF HE'S THE ONE?

The truth is that you won't know for sure until it's almost too late. It's like buying a new lipstick or pair of shoes. How they look and feel in the store can be radically different than they do in your life, day after day. In other words, you don't really know to whom you are married, until you *are* married. But there are plenty of reliable indicators in your courtship that can steer you in the right direction.

In evaluating men, be clear in your own mind about what you *must* have, what you would *like* to have, and what you can probably live without. And be reasonable. My mother used to say *Alles in einem siz nisht do bei keinem*, a Yiddish expression that broadly translates into "All in one is to be found in none." Of course you want a man who is kind and smart, as well as physically, mentally, emotionally, and financially healthy. Every woman does. But think seriously about what you could sacrifice if you had to.

Does he have to be the same religion as you? It helps if he is. Are you willing to move to the west coast so he can pursue a career in the movies? Can you support him while he finishes graduate school? He's a spender, and you're a saver. These are all serious considerations, but not necessarily deal breakers.

You can probably tolerate his never picking up after himself, but how accepting can you be of a man who is untruthful? If he's already lying to you, you'll never be able to trust him. What about a man who always puts his own needs first? Selfishness is almost never *un*learned. Does he minimize your accomplishments to make himself feel superior in the relationship? This will make you insane.

It is human nature to protect what we love. Does he protect you? If his friends or family treat you disrespectfully, does he throw his chest into theirs and demand they apologize to you? If he doesn't, it's a very short road to *him* treating you disrespectfully.

And look at how his father treats his mother. Men get their road map for navigating relationships with women by watching their parents. If his father regards his own wife as a menial, an underling, a servant, the likelihood is that it will be very difficult for him to treat you with the respect that you deserve.

Is he nice to your friends and your family? It's especially important that he treats your parents and siblings with courtesy and hopefully warmth. If he doesn't particularly like your friends, you can probably see them without him. But holidays are spent with family and you don't want to ever have to choose between your husband and your birth family. Of course, some of your family members may need to be reminded that this man is your husband, and if they love you, they will be accepting of and loving toward him.

Okay, here are some deal breakers:

- You want children, but he doesn't. This one is absolutely nonnegotiable. There is no middle ground. Parenthood is a binary condition. You will either have children or you won't. If he doesn't want them and you do—move on. You'll never convince him that he'll love being a dad, and if you want to be a mother, nothing else will take the place of a baby.

- He wants an open marriage. (What? Are you kidding me?)

- He is a substance abuser. Don't think that you will clean him up and set him on the path to sobriety. You won't.

- He has a temper and uses his fists. If he *ever* lays a hand on you in anger—even once—immediately terminate the relationship and never look back.

- Does he fight fair? Even the best relationships experience rocky patches that require conflict resolution skills.

- Does he really listen to your concerns? Or is he interested only in proving how right he is? After you address issues that are causing stress in your relationship, are things usually better? Or does every conversation that includes any criticism of his actions cause an ugly, defensive response? If you regularly walk away from these frustrating talks wishing you never said anything, you need to find a better man with better communication skills who is mature enough to address conflict productively.

As with most things, you should expect to make a few compromises with the man you choose. You have to know who he is at his core and be realistic in your expectations of what about him might improve over time and what will surely not get any better. I know that Lucille, my darling little dachshund, loves me more than almost anything on earth. But she is a food-motivated dog. As much as she loves me, if she had the choice of saving my life or having a piece of chicken, I know I wouldn't fare well in this circumstance. It's unreasonable to expect some things to ever change.

Here are some things that you *can* hope will improve over time: He'll dress better. When he is no longer a student and is required to wear a suit and tie to work, he'll look much more handsome than he did in the torn blue jeans and sloppy T-shirt. He'll wear nicer shoes. He'll shave more closely and get haircuts more regularly. His fingernails may be cleaner. He may lose the extra weight. When he establishes some professional foothold and identity, he'll feel more secure about who he is and that may allow him to be more generous in how he treats you.

But no, he'll never get any smarter. He may learn more things, but his basic cognitive abilities are hardwired by the time you meet him as an adult.

And no, his hair will never grow back, but hair is overrated.

Smart Advice

- You don't really know to whom you are married, until you *are* married.

- Be clear in your own mind about what you *must* have, what you would *like* to have, and what you can probably live without.

- Expect to make a few compromises with the man you choose. He's probably making a few compromises with you as well.

Is It Really Just as Easy to Fall
in Love with a Rich Man?

$\mathcal{E}$VERYONE'S HEARD IT SAID, "IT'S JUST AS EASY TO FALL IN LOVE WITH a rich man as a poor one." It's probably even easier; although when you're in college it's hard to know who among your classmates is actually wealthy. Sometimes your most affluent pals don't even know themselves how prosperous they are. I was recently at a class reunion chatting with a great friend whom I hadn't seen in decades. I asked him what he did professionally, and he told me that he manages a "philanthropy." Huh? Knowing that I'm just a girl from the Bronx, he explained more simply that he gives money away. Again, huh? I asked, "Whose money do you give away?" He answered, "Mine." Thinking that I must not be understanding this properly, I asked, "You've got so much money that your job is giving it away?" He answered, "Yep." I was a bit stunned. As students at Princeton, we all knew that we had many very well-heeled classmates, but I never thought that he was among them. When I shared that with him, he told me that he didn't know it, either, because his parents, wanting him to be industrious, told him of his family's great fortune only when he became an adult.

Before you set upon a mission to find a rich husband, think seriously about what money means to you. Keep in mind that for all that it can buy, it can't protect you, it can't save you, it can't love you, and it can't buy happiness. My mother used to say, "If money can fix it, it's no tragedy." She was a survivor of Auschwitz and knew that the rich Jews suffered just as much as the poor ones. Yes, life can be a little easier if you're rich, but grave illness and infertility aren't impressed with your bank account. Young women who are attracted to the thickness of a wallet regularly seek wealthy older men. Without commenting on whether or not size matters, gold-digging just isn't worth the sacrifice. Wasting one's youth in anticipation of the rapid demise of a rich spouse could result in almost interminable caretaking of the elderly. You are young, smart, and capable—plan to earn your own fortune. If you marry for money, chances are good that when all is said and done, even if you inherit millions, you will have earned it by suppressing your own needs to please a man who holds the purse strings. At best, the value of wealth is that it can give you a few more options. No guarantees, just a few more options.

Attitudes toward money are a stress point in many relationships. If you're a saver and he's a spender, this will be a constant source of conflict. He will resent your frugality and you will be irked by his frivolous use of money. Far from being a sophisticated investor, I have always had a simple financial strategy: Earn as much as possible, spend as little as possible. I take frugality seriously, shopping at three different grocery stores because eggs are cheaper at one store, milk is a few cents less in another, and bread is less expensive at the third. Although I can now afford to shop in one store, this is the routine I've followed ever since I was in my early twenties, living on $9,100 per year. If you weren't born rich, living beneath your means is a key strategy for achieving prosperity. Get in the habit of saving a portion of what you earn—regardless of how little that may be. You need a credit card, but think hard before you plunk it down to pay for an impulse purchase. It is spending real money, but it doesn't feel that way. Paying cash is more likely to make you think before you spend. With the exception of major purchases, the likelihood is that if you don't have the cash to pay for something, you don't need it. Open a bank account in your name and commit yourself to building your savings at every pay period. Life is filled with unexpected incidentals that will cost you. Having a growing repository of your own earnings will make you feel secure and accomplished.

Be sure to carefully check receipts and restaurant checks—they're probably correct, but unless you are independently wealthy, pay attention to what you're being charged for and how your money is being spent. Actually, if you are independently wealthy . . . you've probably been doing this your whole life. And you should understand your paycheck, your bank statements, and your tax return. Again, they are probably correct, but understand what is on them or ask for an explanation of notations and deductions that aren't self-explanatory. Not only do you have a right to know these things, you *should* know them. Personal independence is inextricably liked to financial security, and that security comes from knowing how much money you have, where it is, and how it is being spent.

Paychecks are for adults what report cards are for students. They contain very private information that should *never* be shared with friends. If you don't do as well academically or financially as your peers, you may be thought less of, or even ridiculed. If you do *better* than your friends, they will resent you. Either way, no good comes from the publication of these private measures of success.

Do I even have to say what a bad idea it is to lend money to a friend?

You are not likely to get it back; you will drive yourself crazy trying to, and will probably wind up losing a friend—and your money. When asked for a loan, the answer is simply "I can't do that."

While marrying a rich man or the boss's daughter might be an easy path to financial security, it's just as good—and in fact it is preferable—to marry your socioeconomic equal and as a couple, build your nest egg over time. He who controls the money, controls the relationship. It's better to grow richer together . . . in every sense.

Smart Advice

- Be very clear about what money *is* and what money *isn't*.
- Gold-digging just isn't worth the sacrifice. Better you should earn your own fortune.
- Expect to take care of yourself, in every way. If he provides for you, great! But knowing that you can provide for yourself is even better.

Political Correctness

$\mathcal{S}$o, HOOKUPS ARE FASHIONABLE. SO IS PURSUING A HIGH-POWERED career to the exclusion of all else. And the mere mention of marriage and motherhood among educated young women is positively verboten. Well, are you going to do what's right for you, or are you going to succumb to peer pressure and be politically correct?

You know what? Forget politically correct. Listen to your inner self and do what is right for you, before it's too late.

Regardless of how commonplace and acceptable casual sex is on campus, if you aspire to a more meaningful relationship, don't be goaded into doing anything that isn't right for you. Wait for something better. If marriage and motherhood are at the top of your list, embrace that maternal instinct. Let other women head back to the office weeks after giving birth; if you need to stay home and build LEGO castles with your children instead of climbing the corporate ladder, then that's what you should do. It's a decision you're not likely to regret. Resist the temptation to act out of a need to be seen as politically correct if it is inconsistent with what you know is best for you. If others are unwilling to accept your choices, then quite simply they are not worthy of you.

I was born without a "politically correct" gene. As much as it might matter to be accepted as a fully integrated part of the "in crowd," it doesn't usually work out that way for me. Strongly opinionated, I was never willing to subjugate my personal beliefs in favor of the prevailing zeitgeist. I'm still not. The trade-off just doesn't seem worth it. Popularity at the expense of authenticity? Nope. Fitting in is good, but being an outlier isn't so bad.

Even the term *politically correct* just doesn't sound right. Correct is *correct*. It's a simple word that needs no modifier. It means that something is free from error, and in accordance with fact and truth. It's the opposite of a mistake. Why ever would a word as straightforward as this need an explanatory adjective? It doesn't. Again, correct is just . . . correct. Politically correct means something else. It means *wrong*— cloaked in a tacit acceptance of these untruths by spineless people hoping to look benevolent, forward-thinking, and progressive. It means "not *really* correct" in the same way that *almost* won means lost, and *nearly* done means unfinished.

When our personal beliefs are in contrast to popular opinion, it requires strength and courage to remain true to ourselves. This dilemma can start very early in life, in the form of piling on the unfortunate kid who is regularly picked on by the grade school illuminati. Ridiculing the schoolyard misfits that you actually like, because the cool kids regularly tease them and you want to curry their favor, is obviously acting badly for the sake of popularity. Don't be ingenuous; if you know it's wrong, don't be brainwashed into thinking that there is absolution in being politically correct. There isn't. Be a better person than that.

The brainwashing of the very young also reaches into the classroom. Regardless of the trend towards anti-intellectualism, you know that smart *is* cool. In fact, it is the coolest, except among the underachievers who will always feel threatened by the thinkers. Why would you even bother to seek their approval? The cynics, the snobs, the ignorant, the atheists, the egotists—they are lacking in substance but thrive on being politically correct.

The approval of others is of course comforting and validating, but at what cost? Throughout your life, make the decisions that are right for *you*. "It's just not *done*" is never a good reason to opt out of anything. And "It's what *everyone* is doing" is a terrible excuse for inexcusable behavior.

When I was an expectant mother for the first time in 1988, natural childbirth without drugs was considered the *only* way to deliver your baby. Thankfully, my best friend had her baby boy six months before I had mine and she shared with me this most important of all advice for pregnant women: "When they wheel you into the labor and delivery room at the hospital, and the doctor asks if you want an epidural, the answer is 'Yes, yes, I want an epidural. Please give me an epidural.' " She was so right. Since then, I've shared this sage advice with every pregnant woman I've known.

Okay, so I delivered a very big (eight pounds, four ounces), healthy baby boy and then the breastfeeding earth mothers of La Leche League were insisting that I nurse my son. La Leche is an international nonprofit organization that distributes information and promotes breastfeeding. It was what *all* new mothers were doing. I hated it, wasn't good at it, and my baby didn't seem to take to it, either. I kept trying because it was the politically correct thing to do, but it didn't get better until I spoke with my pediatrician, who assured me that our entire generation grew up on bottle-fed formula. Of course! I forgot that I could choose to do something different than what every other mother was doing. So I buttoned my blouse, bought a case of Enfamil, and happily bottle-fed my bouncing baby boy. It was better for him and better for me.

My second son was born within months of the birth of the second child of all of my friends. They then all needed another bedroom and moved out of Manhattan for the space that the suburbs offered. I'm a city girl and refused to make that move. I bought the apartment next to mine and raised my boys on the Upper East Side. They never had a backyard that I could see from my kitchen window, but they had Central Park, the Metropolitan Museum of Art, Broadway, and everything else that makes New York City the center of the universe.

I am a product of New York City public schools, from kindergarten until the time I matriculated at Princeton University. When my children were five years old, they started kindergarten at P.S. 158 on Seventy-Seventh Street at York Avenue. *None* of my friends sent their children to public school, but I was confident that if I instilled in them an appreciation for the importance of education, they would do well and earn their place in the best universities. I did, and so did they. I don't think that any of my friends' private school, prep school progenies made it to the Ivy League.

Being politically correct is for people who care more about style than substance. Of course, it is easy to go with the flow and follow the crowd, but don't do it if the crowd is going in a direction that doesn't suit you.

Smart Advice

- Have the strength and courage to remain true to yourself.

- Being an outlier isn't so bad, if it's who you are.

- *Correct* needs no modifier. *Politically correct* means wrong.

Are You a Little Hothouse Tomato?

*N*OBODY LOVES LITTLE HOTHOUSE TOMATOES. NO, NOT THE JUICY, red salad additions, but people who are so high-strung and high-maintenance that one wonders how they get though the day. It must start very early in childhood, because you sometimes see it in little princess girls who walk into a room, look around, and scream for no apparent reason. They are compelled to constantly create big drama around them everywhere they go. It's hard to understand whether they are needlessly terrified or just craving attention. Either way, it's not good.

You already know whether you are this kind of princess. The crying theatrics that punctuate most of your days are a pretty good indicator that you are a little hothouse tomato. Think seriously about an attitude makeover. If you are addicted to overreaction, you will repel the sane, thoughtful, conscientious men whom you will want to attract. The best men look for women who are confident, capable, and grounded in reality. As the future mother to his children, a wife who can *comfort* a crying child, not be one, is what a man wants.

The fabric of good marriage is woven from mutual trust and a belief that you can count on your spouse to be there for you when things go wrong. It's the *poorer, worse,* and *sickness* components that are included in most marriage vows. While we all hope for *richer, better,* and *health,* a certain amount of adversity has to be expected and can hopefully be handled with grace. What is *not* part of the marriage contract is the endless and needless dramas created by the little hothouse tomatoes who have absolutely no ability to withstand the most minor disappointment. Even worse is when no actual catastrophe has occurred, but they need that comforting attention so desperately that they will create tragedy out of nothing. When evaluating possible life partners, look at their coping mechanisms. You don't want to be that pitiful spouse who is relegated to indulging these endless psychodramas. Life is filled with episodes and occurrences that are less than ideal.

The hothouse tomato has no ability to deal with the slightest temperature fluctuations or any other deviation from their expectations. They have no resilience, they have no grit; they are selfish, disingenuous, and draining. Don't be one, and definitely don't marry one!

Conversely, everyone loves people with grit. They are positive, industrious, committed individuals who wake up each morning believing that every day offers opportunities for success—despite yesterday's setbacks. They are inspiring. Instead of responding to misfortune with passive resistance, they offer proactive defiance. And people with grit are in the race for the long haul. They are the marathon runners, not the sprinters. When you search for your life partner, look for someone with this kind of staying power. You'll want someone who despite adversity can always get up off the mat and go on confidently, positively, and cheerfully.

The hothouse tomatoes are fundamentally lacking in self-confidence, perseverance, faith that they are good enough, and the understanding that bumps in the road are just that—temporary setbacks. We are resilient by nature, and to a greater or lesser degree all have the ability to recover from difficult situations. You have to trust that better times are on the way, and keep your wits about you and maintain a good spirit until they arrive.

Some newborns learn how to self-soothe in a matter of weeks. They calm down each night and allow themselves to fall asleep peacefully with an instinctive, innocent confidence that the sun will rise again soon and with it will come a loving parent, a clean diaper, and milk. These babies are a joy. Young women who are composed, calm, and confident are also a joy and they attract the best men.

Sadly, many women are so invested in their psychodramas that they are oblivious to the fact that they are little hothouse tomatoes. Before you dismiss the possibility that this is you, ask yourself if you are constantly complaining and regularly disappointed when you compare your current situation with your mythical past or prophetic future. If you don't like your friends, your family, your home, your clothes, your body, your life . . . chances are you belong in a heated building designed for rearing delicate plants. Snap out of it! Stop whining. Stop complaining.

When I was a very young girl I remember crying inconsolably to my mother because a boy had broken my heart, my best friend had become someone else's best friend, and the popular girls at school were being mean to me. My mother told me that if all the people in the world sat around a big table and put their troubles out in front of them such that you could see the sufferings of everyone else, you would grab your own back and run away happily.

Learn to love yourself and your life, and live your best life today and every day. Even if things aren't perfect, get happy with what you've got. There's not always something better.

You have to know a good thing when you've got it.

Smart Advice

- Young women who are composed, calm, and confident attract the best men.
- If you are a little hothouse tomato, think seriously about an attitude makeover.
- Snap out of it! Stop whining! Stop complaining! It's so unattractive.

Where Is Love?

$\mathcal{A}$NY THINKING PERSON WOULD AGREE THAT TO REALIZE ONE'S PRO-
fessional aspirations requires serious forethought, planning, and stead-
fast dedication. How is it that many of those same people, when asked
about finding a spouse, will wistfully reply, "Oh, love just . . . happens"?

No, it doesn't. Nothing just happens. Obviously, finding the right
man is a crucial component to fulfilling the dream of a traditional marriage and family. Why would any woman leave something as important
as that to chance?

Smarten up, girl!

Finding the love of your life requires embarking upon a methodical search. Consider seriously where you are likely to find men who are
mostly age-appropriate, mostly single, and likely to share your same history of accomplishment and intellectual curiosity—essential criteria of
compatibility.

Forget what you've seen on television. You won't find the man of
your dreams in the supermarket. You might, but the odds aren't in
your favor and you know almost nothing about the guy squeezing mel-

ons, other than what you can discern from looking in his shopping cart. Your college campus is an obvious and very reasonable place to look. If you've already graduated, get involved with alumni activities. You know that at least you share an academic credential; maybe you share more than that. Or maybe your clergy can make an appropriate introduction at your house of worship. Approach the search for a wonderful mate as systematically as you would search for a great job. You'll probably have several jobs in your lifetime. Hopefully you'll have only one husband. Invest your very best and most focused efforts toward finding the right man.

How will you know when you have found true love? We are all so influenced by the media that we have absurd ideas of what love looks like. We've romanticized the tragic lovers: Cathy & Heathcliff, Romeo & Juliet, Tony & Maria. We've loved being entertained by the lovers who were never meant to be: Scarlett & Rhett, Porgy & Bess. Hollywood has even romanticized abusive men like Billy Bigelow in *Carousel* and Stanley Kowalski in *A Streetcar Named Desire*. We've almost forgotten that when stars are not aligned, tragedy ensues—it's the epitome of unlucky, not love. Love shouldn't end in devastation or annihilation, and it almost never happens at first sight—that's usually lust, and don't confuse the two.

So what *does* love really look like? It looks different for everybody, and the elements of attraction have been fodder for sociologists for ages. But if you are looking in the right places for people with whom you share core values and experiences, it's likely that you'll find your match. Remember that love grows over time. Among people with whom you share fundamental commonalities, it's amazing how you can learn to love almost anybody.

If my mother ever talked with me about finding a husband, I don't remember it. I *do* recall her telling me about the weddings that took place in the displaced persons camps after the liberation. My parents are both survivors of concentration camps. My mother was in Auschwitz; my father was liberated from Bergen-Belsen in 1945. They were married in a DP camp in November 1946. She told me of another female survivor and friend of hers at the time who said, "I'm getting married the week after next—either to this one, or that one, I'm not sure—but I'm getting married the week after next." After all they had been through, they didn't want to be alone. Nor was there much to differentiate one potential husband from another. They were all penniless, orphaned, and struggling to regain their physical and mental health. Building a new life was more easily done with someone—*anyone*. Among the people I know like my parents who married in DP camps and came to the United States, I don't know of a single divorce.

Our notion of love has been distorted, complicated, and diminished by high-profile philanderers, some of whom have had the amazing good fortune to be married to women who stand by their man despite their dalliances. Again, this is not what you want. If a man can't be faithful to you while you are seriously dating, then he can't be trusted to be a faithful husband. Move on.

Once you have your basic criteria met, evaluate potential mates on whether or not they will put *your* needs before their own, and if you can put *their* needs before your own. I remember a rabbi telling a bride and groom that the key to a good marriage is to give your spouse everything you have to give, and more . . . and take only what you need. Very good advice, but it necessitates both parties' commitment to be selfless. It's asking a lot, but it's that kind of love that can sustain a couple for better or worse, richer or poorer, through sickness and health until death do them part. When you're very young and healthy, it's hard to imagine life's challenges, but ask any long-married couple—even the happiest unions need a coping mechanism for when things go wrong. You can overcome almost any adversity as a couple when you know that your partner puts your needs before his own.

If you must use movie romances as a template for finding the right man, think about a cocker spaniel named Lady and a mutt called Tramp and a candlelit spaghetti dinner.

Answer honestly . . . would the man you're dating push his meatball to your side of the plate?

If you know that he would . . . he's THE ONE.

Smart Advice

- Love doesn't just happen. Nothing just happens. You have to plan for it.
- Your college campus is an obvious and very reasonable place to look for the love of your life.
- You can learn to love almost anybody with whom you share core commonalities.

Behaving Badly

*W*E ALL OCCASIONALLY HAVE LAPSES IN JUDGMENT AND DO STUPID things that in retrospect we regret. Sometimes we just act without thinking, or out of curiosity, or because we think that we can get away with being a *little* bit bad. And most of the time, if we are only minimally inappropriate, our transgressions will be forgiven and forgotten. Here's what you can't realistically hope to have disappear from anyone's memory—let along from their Facebook, Instagram, or Pinterest pages—anytime soon: you, stumbling out of a party either too drunk or too high to remember how to put one foot in front of another. And if you've been overserved to the point that you are vomiting on yourself or others, this too is an unfortunate image that has staying power. Think about this . . . an obviously drunk woman offends almost every sense. She looks awful, slurred speech is a turnoff, puked-on clothes and matted hair—ugh. And the smell! The scent of your perfume should linger, not the stench of upchuck. Drunken sorority girls are objects of ridicule. Be smart about managing your alcoholic consumption . . . and your image!

Experimentation is a cornerstone of youth. One of the great joys of newfound independence is testing one's limits and venturing down paths that were heretofore forbidden. But with independence comes responsibility. If you are going to act stupidly, know that there could be consequences, some of which could stay with you and damage your reputation in perpetuity.

If you are compelled to engage in questionable behavior, at least be discreet about it. The walk of shame as you sneak out of his apartment on Sunday morning in high heels and a sparkly sequin dress is the equivalent of wearing a sandwich sign saying, "I just spent the night having sex with a man who isn't my husband!"

No, it's not illegal, and you're not branded with a scarlet *A*, unless of course you are a married woman with a man other than your husband, but it may cause you to be viewed by others in a less than desirable light.

Do not even *think* about attributing your embarrassing behavior to having drunk too much. In the light of day, you may not feel good about what you did, but the likelihood is that you did exactly what you wanted to do—but may not have had the courage to do in a completely sober state. Drunkenness can make you feel freer in your actions, but it won't move you to act in a manner that is wholly inconsistent with who you are, even if you are almost unconscious.

And if you are passed out drunk . . . what are you thinking? Surely you are well aware of the physical problems associated with excessive drinking: alcohol poisoning, cirrhosis of the liver, hypertension, heart disease, sleep disorders, depression, to name a few. But beyond the medical risks associated with regular drunkenness, it's an invitation to be taken advantage of—especially for women. Why would you *ever* put yourself in a position where you are out of control? This is a disaster waiting to happen. If you are too drunk to speak, then you may be incapable of saying *no* or warding off unwanted advances. And then it's all on you. Please spare me your "blaming the victim" outrage. If you are provocatively dressed, drink too much, and knowingly (or unknowingly) wander into an eager young man's room, then you have displayed screamingly bad judgment and must bear accountability for what may happen next. This is not just some youthful indiscretion—it is absolute stupidity. You are putting yourself at risk, possibly serious risk. Most women, due to the sheer size differential, start out physically disadvantaged in a tussle with men. In a drunken state, women's vulnerability is exacerbated exponentially. This is a situation that is intrinsically lacking equality. Girls, you have to smarten up about this and protect yourself. You are ultimately responsible for keeping your wits about you and ensuring your own safety in *all* situations.

Even worse than acting badly because you were under the influence of behavior-altering substances is trying to explain it away by saying things like "I was so drunk, I don't even remember what I did last night!" Nonsense. You most certainly do know what you did last night—and so does everyone else. Attempting to hide behind drunkenness is never believable—it's delusional. You are adding insult to injury by feebly trying to eradicate the reality of your actions by lying about them. Nobody will believe you, and your unwillingness to accept responsibility for your own actions makes you look even worse than a trollop—it makes you look like an untruthful trollop.

Young people have to be smarter for themselves in social settings that include drinking and possible drug use. You *really* have to be smarter than drinking beyond your limit and risking being drugged or used sexually against your wishes. And young men also have to be smarter about how much they drink and how it affects them. The line between a drunken hookup and a sexual assault is very thin, but the charge of rape, regardless of the circumstance, is substantial.

Always be in control of your faculties; know where you are and whom you are with and be capable of making intelligent decisions for yourself. There are those rare occasions when you are with people whom you trust so completely that you allow yourself to cross that line of consciousness, just to see what it feels like. Again, we grow and learn through experimentation. But be smart for yourself—stumbling drunk isn't attractive and being so high that you have gaps in your memory can be disastrous. Know your limits and be sure that you remain sober enough; straight enough to be aware of what is going on around you and to protect yourself.

Smart Advice

- Manage your image smartly. Be discreet and exercise good judgment.
- Drunkenness is an invitation to be taken advantage of— especially for women.
- You are *always* responsible for your own actions and your own safety. Sober up!

Guilt—You Do It to Yourself

*T*HE EXPECTATIONS OF AN ARDENT SUITOR—REGARDLESS OF THE lovely gift or expensive dinner he bought you—are *his* expectations. They don't oblige you to do anything that you don't want to do. Don't be bullied, and don't be guilted into going further on a date than your comfort zone will allow. Decades ago, young men would regularly complain to young women who curtailed intimacy on their dates that they were experiencing a *colorful* condition—a temporary fluid congestion in the genital region, accompanied by acute testicular pain caused by prolonged and unsatisfied sexual arousal. Please. Have no pity on these men for their masculine aching, but only for their artless attempt at guilting women into having premature sex with them.

There is an old story about a mother who gives her young daughter two scarves for Hanukkah. The girl takes one of them out of the gift box, decoratively wraps it around her neck, and asks, "Ma! Doesn't this look pretty?" To which the mother says, "What . . . You don't like the *other* one?"

Admittedly, I found this story much funnier before I had my own children. Perhaps it is because I was unaware of how important it is for mothers to receive validation from their children. I always thought it was the other way around. Either way, there is no part of this scenario that merits feelings of guilt. The answer to the mother's guilt-baiting question is "Yes, Ma . . . I do like the other scarf, but I can only wear one at a time." No cause for guilt. The manufactured pain on Mom's face is . . . manufactured by Mom, and not caused by her daughter's acting unreasonably.

When you've knowingly committed an offense, you will and should feel guilty . . . because you *are* guilty. You know when you've done the wrong thing—your conscience will remind you, and karma's a bitch, especially if you *are* one. But if you are a person of honesty and integrity, you will make amends, issue sincere apologies, and commit yourself to doing better moving forward.

Guilt is a powerful motivator, but it is a self-generated emotion. Do what you have to do; as long as your intent isn't to hurt others, there's nothing to feel guilty about. Of course, sometimes even the most considerate people will unintentionally be hurtful to others, and ancillary damage requires an apology or restitution, but it does not merit guilt. If you've restored the injured party for whatever actual loss may have occurred, and expressed sincere regrets for any inconvenience or perceived insult, then you've done what you needed to do. Move on, and don't allow yourself to be held back by unearned shame or regret.

Don't feel guilty about acting in your own self-interest. It's what you are supposed to do. Ultimately, we are each responsible for our own happiness and it is unreasonable to think that validation and fulfillment is an external bestowal. The exception, of course, is parents, especially the parents of young children. But unlike the example in the scarf story, it is not a child's job to selflessly placate and nurture parents; rather it is the other way around. A child's happiness, success, and independence should be satisfaction enough for any good mother. The martyrization of parenthood, embodied in absurd statements like "I gave my *life* for you," is little more than blatant guilt laying. Obviously, a parent who regularly utters such selfish nonsense did *not* give their life for anyone. That life remains very much their own, here on earth. Recognize these oppressive statements as cries for attention, and respond kindly, but don't allow yourself to be manipulated by these ploys—not by a family member, and definitely not by a date.

Unless you have acted with malice aforethought, don't feel that you have done wrong or failed in an obligation. Taking care of your own needs is normal, natural, and usually the right thing to do. Dogs do this instinctively. They might look guilty if they have an accident on the living room floor, but not when they beg for food at the dinner table—they are hungry. They will almost knock you down when you walk in the door at the end of the day because they miss you and love you. They exhibit no guilt over showing affection, regardless of how overwhelming it might be.

There is a story about a dog who wandered into a neighbor's backyard on a summer's afternoon. When the neighbor went inside, the dog sweetly followed after him, curled himself up in a carpeted corner, and took a nap. After about an hour, the dog followed the man back outside and presumably went home. The next afternoon, the dog came back and again followed the man into the house and took a nap. After several days of the same thing happening, the man attached a note to the dog's collar saying that the dog was welcome to come visit in the afternoons and take a nap in his home, but he just wanted to be sure that the owners knew where the dog was. The next day, the dog came back with a note from the owners saying that they were wondering where their dog had wandered off to every afternoon, but they had four children under five years old and now understood that the dog just needed a quiet hour to sleep.

Animals instinctively know how to take care of themselves, sometimes better than humans.

We allow ourselves to act out of feeling guilty. Usually it is unfounded guilt and the result of the manipulation of others who are looking to satisfy their own needs. Don't let anyone guilt you into doing anything that isn't right for you or that you are uncomfortable with.

You know . . . it's taken me months to write these words for *your* benefit. Maybe you should *take* my advice? I only want the *best* for you.

Smart Advice

- If you act honestly and decently, you have no reason to feel guilty. Others will have to learn to deal with their disappointment in you.
- Don't feel guilty about acting in your own self-interest.
- Don't let anyone (men) use guilt to manipulate you into doing anything (having sex) if you don't want to.

Plan for Reality

*P*LANNING FOR YOUR PERSONAL HAPPINESS IS SO, WELL... personal, that women sometimes get all caught up in the emotion of it and lose sight of the realities. It's critical that you approach this most important of missions with logic and reason. There are facts that you must consider, but equally important are the things that you just know instinctively—you've always known.

If having children is an essential component of your life plan for happiness, you have to embrace soberly the limitations on your own ability to conceive and deliver healthy babies. There are endless articles written by doctors and scientists that talk about fertility rates, and every study tweaks the information a little differently. Because we so want this to go our way, the temptation is to pick the articles and studies that put our personal situation in the most hopeful light. Don't get caught up on the statistics—let common sense be your guide. You know that you put your life goals at risk by putting off having babies until after you've established your career.

Women have a limited number of years within which they can bear children. Period. You are in your biological prime to procreate between the ages of sixteen and twenty-eight, but the earlier you get to it, the better your chances are to deliver healthy children. Visit your ob-gyn after age thirty-five and your file is marked "AMA," or Advanced Maternal Age. This very specifically applies to the complications older women face getting pregnant. It doesn't even begin to address the higher risk for chromosomal abnormalities faced by older women who are lucky enough to achieve conception. Here's another reality . . . when a woman is forty years of age, the risk of having a Down syndrome baby is 1 in 60, compared with 1 in 1,500 when she is twenty-five. Being pregnant at an advanced age poses risks to the mother as well as to the baby. By being older, a pregnant woman has a greater likelihood to develop medical disorders such as diabetes, hypertensive disorders, or fibroids, all of which can affect pregnancy and birth.

In your twenties your ovaries still have a relatively good number of eggs, which is why you have a greater chance of becoming pregnant. And in your twenties a greater percentage of those eggs are genetically normal. At birth, a woman is born with all of the eggs that she will have in her lifetime, approximately four hundred. If a woman releases one egg every twenty-eight days, that's thirteen eggs per year. If the onset of menses begins at eleven years old but she doesn't start thinking about getting pregnant until she is twenty-six, that's almost half of her eggs gone before she has even considered having a child. Every childbearing year that passes, there are fewer eggs left, and the percentage of those remaining eggs that are genetically normal decreases. These are the simple facts of why women have a decreasing fertility rate, increased miscarriage rate, and increased chance of birth defects as they get older. At thirty years old, fewer than 50 percent of your remaining eggs are considered normal, and your risk of miscarriage is about 20 percent. By thirty-five years old, only 25 percent of your remaining eggs are normal.

The quality of men's sperm also deteriorates somewhat over time, but not to nearly the same degree as women's eggs, nor does this significantly impact their ability to father children. Most men can ejaculate at will and replenish their lost sperm overnight. Women can't replace their lost eggs, nor can they ovulate on command.

These are biological realities, not a statement on older women's strength, values, goodness, or intelligence. It's just the way it is. If you want to bear your own children, be very cognizant of how your ability to conceive and deliver healthy babies diminishes dramatically if you wait too long.

If you miss your window of opportunity to bear your own children the old-fashioned way, you could sadly come to accept that you will never have the children you hoped for. Or you might consider many of the other options to motherhood. If you have the wherewithal to anticipate your needs, you could freeze your eggs in your early thirties at a cost of around $15,000 to harvest and an annual storage fee of $500. Or you could try to find a surrogate. Or you could consider becoming a single mother. Or you could prepare yourself for the trauma, expense, and frequent disappointment of in vitro fertilization. IVF is the most successful infertility treatment available, and the pregnancy rate is only about 10 percent per try. The cost of each IVF attempt is around $15,000–$20,000. Would you consider an egg donor? Do you have $30,000 to explore that option? Maybe you could adopt. That also could cost upwards of $30,000 and usually takes years.

But why would you put yourself through the trauma, expense, and frequent disappointment associated with any of these options? In addition to teaching young women the mechanics of safe sex, we should probably also be teaching them about the risks and realities of prolonging their foray into motherhood.

Start looking for a husband early and plan to have your children young enough to avoid the nightmare of infertility treatments or the heartbreak of childlessness. Taking care of young children requires energy. In your forties, you won't have the stamina or patience that you had in your twenties and thirties. Think seriously about having your babies while you are able to be with them enthusiastically and energetically. And think about your grandchildren! You will want to be young enough to enjoy them, and around long enough for them to get to know you.

My grandparents perished long before I was born. I had friends who had grandparents who were actually in their fifties, but in my preteen eyes I thought they were one hundred. We are definitely aging better than we did decades ago.

Brooklyn may be the new Manhattan (it really isn't), brown may be the new black, but regardless of how much better we may look, regarding your reproductive system . . . forty is *not* the new thirty.

Smart Advice

- You're smarter to put your career on hold and have your babies, than putting off having babies until after you've established your career.

- Pregnancy at an advanced age poses risks to the mother as well as to the baby.

- Attempting to have children other than the old-fashioned way is fraught with disappointment. You have to be very rich, very lucky, and very patient. Don't count on it.

PART III

Your Thirties

All right. You're in your thirties now, and now you know that life can be tough and your plans don't always work out. You've won some and you've lost some.

The realities of not being a kid anymore can be sobering, but you are smarter now than you've ever been.

Right?

Right.

Armed with the wisdom gained from years of experience, you can look forward with a confidence that you may not have had in your teens or twenties.

So, a Thirty-Five-Year-Old Single Person Walks into a Cocktail Party . . .

*H*OW DOES THE STORY GO? IT ALL DEPENDS ON WHETHER YOU ARE A single man or a single woman. They are two radically different stories.

If you are a bachelor, you are as welcome as flowers that bloom in the spring. Your hostess is *so* delighted to have a single man at her soirée! There are never enough eligible bachelors to go around! She may even have a daughter she'd like to introduce you to! Or maybe she has an unmarried younger sister, or a niece. The possibilities are endless. Your host is also thrilled to have another guy at the party with whom to talk about man stuff, and if he's an old married man, he would love to relive his glorious premarriage days vicariously through tales of your bachelor exploits. Single women at the event won't be able to take their eyes off you. They will whisper among themselves about how much they would love to be introduced to you. If there are other unmarried men at the party, they will be happy to share the wealth, and some will even act as your wingman if there is a woman in attendance whom you may want to get to know.

Thirty-five-year-old single gals don't receive nearly as many invitations to cocktail parties (or anything else) as single men. They are usually as welcome as a skunk at a lawn party. Hostesses of these soirées will shun the older unmarried woman. They don't want you anywhere near their husbands: They sense that you are desperate to find a man—even if you aren't! Everyone *knows* you are.

Their husbands may find you interesting and attractive, but the wives will see to it that you are kept separate. They may have unmarried daughters and certainly don't want *their* girls competing with you for the few single men. The other single women at the cocktail party will be assessing and comparing your relative attractiveness to their own, but if they are also in their mid-thirties, it won't matter. The single men at the party will have little or no interest in *any* of you—they are interested in women who are in their twenties.

So you and the other spinsters-in-training can drown your sorrows in another cocktail and then share a cab home to the Upper West Side.

The difference between being a mid-thirties single man and a mid-thirties single woman is that one is an object of desire, and the other is an object of pity. For unmarried women, a single man in his mid-thirties is, as Aeschylus wrote, "like land to sailors long at sea." So welcome, so wonderful, so hopefully anticipated. For unattached men, the universe of available and interested women is almost unlimited and they can take all the time in the world to pick a lucky lady. They know that the world is their oyster and their possibilities are endless. Who wouldn't want to be around that kind of happiness and positive energy?

Single thirty-five-year-old women know that they have probably missed their opportunity to find a husband, and almost certainly have lost their chance to bear their own children. These women live with profound disappointment. This visible dissatisfaction can get in the way of their finding happiness, and it can make others uncomfortable around them. It goes without saying that not *all* women want to be married or mothers, but for women who want both, they have to plan for these essential elements of their life's happiness with dedication. And they must do so early enough to course-correct if necessary, lest they wind up being regarded much like the porcupine at a nudist colony. Needless to say, unmarried women with no children can lead extraordinarily fulfilling lives. But if a woman's heartfelt dream is to have a traditional family, all else is a consolation prize.

Sadly, there isn't much hopeful news for thirty-five-year-old single women who want a family, and they are painfully aware of that. The rules of dating, mating, and courtship have changed in ways that benefit young men but hurt young women. Girls who know that they are on their last pint of nubile fuel should go into overdrive to find a husband and start a family. Even if he isn't the man of your dreams, if in wedlock you can conceive a healthy child, then you will at least have fulfilled the dream of motherhood. And he might surprise you and actually be more of a Prince Charming than you thought. Don't call it "settling." Call it "settling smart." Sometimes we have to take less than everything we hoped for and be patient. It's amazing how things have a way of working out. Just as some marriages of the most besotted lovers end, unions of less infatuated partners can grow and become great romances. Is it really good advice to have a child with a man who is less than the love of your life? If bearing your own children is your single most important goal—then, yes, it is very good advice. And you might find that Mr. Good Enough is actually a pretty great guy. Regardless of how your marriage ends, you will love your child forever, and you may meet a wonderful man in your forties, fifties, or even at the nursing home's shuffleboard court. But if you miss your chance to be pregnant and deliver your child, then that dream is off the table forever.

Don't let the astronomical divorce rates turn you off to marriage or cause you to delay getting married. It's hard to know exactly what is the secret sauce that keeps some couples together forever, but it is missing from the majority of marriages that fail. The best you can do is choose your mate wisely, commit yourself to making your union successful, and start early enough to modify your plan if necessary.

If it just doesn't happen for you, and you don't meet a suitable husband soon enough to start a traditional family, at a certain point you will have to stop looking for THE ONE and commit yourself to thinking about what's going to make you happiest with the choices that *are* available to you.

Smart Advice

- If you are a single woman in your thirties, redouble your efforts to find THE ONE before it's too late.
- We don't always get everything we want all at once. Be purposeful but patient.
- In the absence of Mr. Right, settling for Mr. Good Enough is "settling smart."

Tell Me What You Want . . .
What You Really, *Really* Want

$\mathcal{T}$HE EASIEST THING TO DO IS WHAT EVERYONE ELSE DOES. THE PATH of least resistance has always been to do whatever is politically popular. In the seventies, when the fashion was to adorn your long, straight hair with beads and breastfeed your baby in public, you found lots of validation among your women friends to do so. Or, when burning your bra and wearing miniskirts was the style, you could have easily joined the crowd of bare-legged women around the Maidenform bonfire while incinerating your C-cups. These are silly, transient things that may stay with you as colorful memories, or very minor points of embarrassment, but they are short-lived and won't change your life.

Following the current trend for highly educated women, which is to delay marriage for a decade after graduation while pursuing a career, may very well be an unforgiving and unforgivably bad, life-changing decision. If you truly do not want to navigate your twenties with a partner, then don't. Some people feel that they can't manage a serious relationship while starting to build a professional life. I really don't understand why not. As I said earlier, your partner/spouse/boyfriend should be an enhancement to your life, not a drain on it. If you've selected your partner well, it is a huge comfort and benefit to know that at the end of a long workday, you have someone who is committed to you and with whom you can share your daily triumphs and frustrations. But if you want to singularly focus on your career, then . . . good luck!

However, if you are *as* committed to your *personal* happiness as you are to your professional success, I urge you to listen to your inner self and reject the preaching of those who would have you exclusively invested in work. Everyone finds work . . . eventually. Some people discover their extreme skills and ideal career path earlier in their work life and some later, but everyone who wants to work does find work.

Sadly, not everyone who wants marriage and parenthood finds a spouse or bears children. If you know that marriage and family are a significant component of your life plan for happiness, you absolutely must make finding a partner a priority—much more so than the development of your career. You'll work. I can almost guarantee that you'll work. But honestly, until you find a spouse, I would advise you invest your effort and energy at least 75 percent in searching for a partner and 25 percent in professional development.

You can always make up for lost time and reduced effort on the job. However, if you delay searching for a spouse, you may find that you've waited too long. The men you want to marry are already married. You won't be able to compete with women ten years younger than you. And your eggs will have passed their expiration date.

Okay, let's be honest. Try to turn off the external voices that are attempting to influence your thinking and move you in a direction that may be supporting their agenda, but not your own. This is hard. If what you want is not politically popular, it requires true grit to be true to yourself. But nothing can be more important in achieving your life's goals than for you to know who you are and what will *honestly* make you happy. If you can define your goals and hold fast to them, then you can be purposeful in how you approach every day and your successes will be measurable. There may be something to be said for Napoleon's battle plan—"Show up, see what happens"—but perhaps the quest for your personal happiness requires a bit more methodical planning than Napoleon's did in his quest to conquer the Russian army. This haphazard plan didn't serve Napoleon well in 1812, and it probably won't serve you any better today.

You may not want to marry a man. You may want to marry a woman. Or you may not want to marry at all. You may want to be married but not have children. Whatever it is that you want, *own it*, and don't let anyone make you feel like there is anything wrong with you or the life that you choose for yourself. Think seriously about whether you want children at all. It's not for everyone. From the time I was a very young girl, I knew that I wanted to be married, live in Manhattan, do something professionally creative, host wonderful dinner parties, learn to knit, visit Paris, and become a great cook. But there was nothing that I knew with *greater* certainty than that I wanted babies. Oscar Wilde was wrong when he said that "the two greatest disappointments in life are not getting your heart's desire—and getting it." Motherhood was exactly what I wanted and it is truly better than anything I could have ever imagined.

Remember that having children is one of the only decisions you'll ever make that can't be undone—along with committing suicide. From my perspective, the former is the best thing you could ever do. The latter is the worst, but they are both irreversible decisions. If you want to have babies, you have to plan for it much sooner than you may think.

Work. Do you work because you have to, or do you work because you want to? If you work in order to maintain a summer home in Montauk and continue to winter in Gstaad, then you don't really have to work. You love to work—and you love the grand stuff that working affords you. It's all good, but be honest (at least with yourself) about the choices you make and why you make them. To say that you *have* to work is an insult to women who *really* do have to work: single mothers and other women who, through whatever circumstance, are the sole or joint supporter of their household. "I work because I have to" means that if you didn't work, there wouldn't be food on the table or there wouldn't be a roof over your head. It doesn't mean that you would have to go without the latest fashions, dining at the most fashionable restaurants, or vacationing in the most luxurious resorts.

To some degree, you *are* what happens to you, but mostly you are what you choose to become. And choosing wisely requires that you listen to your inner self and be very clear about what you want . . . what you really, *really* want.

Smart Advice

- For the most part, you are what you choose to become.
- Be true to yourself and honest about what you want.
- Until you find a spouse, invest most of your energy in searching for a partner.

Do It Yourself

$\mathcal{T}$HE CORE OF SELF-SUFFICIENCY IS THE ABILITY TO DO FOR ONESELF, make for oneself, and care for oneself. The common admonition of parents and teachers to young people is "Make something useful *of yourself*." Of course, that is very good advice. But I'm advocating something more. Make something, do something, create something by yourself and for yourself. Literally, *make* something useful.

We live in a society where we buy everything ready-made. Successful people who have the means will pay others to perform the tasks that define their lives. They pay nannies to care for their children, housekeepers to care for their home and prepare their meals, and landscapers to plant their gardens. Why would you relinquish these experiences to others? They are some of life's greatest joys. It would seem that the mark of *true* success would be to pay others to do everything else so that you could be with your children, in the comfort of your home, making dinner for your family and planting flowers in your backyard.

We've moved so far away from an industrial mind-set that the simple pleasures and satisfaction of creating something from scratch have all but vanished from our lives. Almost nobody aspires to being a shoemaker or a milliner anymore, but how satisfying must it be to make a perfect pair of shoes, or create a spectacular hat. Okay, with the exception of royal weddings, there's not a lot of hats to be found these days, but the value of making something with your own hands is tremendously meaningful and can be a lasting identifier of who you are—an heirloom.

The Metropolitan Museum of Art has a wonderful collection of stitched samplers made by young, unmarried women in colonial America. At a time when a girl was expected to find an appropriate man, get married, have children, and take care of home and family, these embroidered cloths reflected the values and talents of the girl and her family to potential husbands. At that time, boys were educated in traditional academic subjects, while a girl's education might have included basic reading and math but was much more focused on the skills that would serve her as a wife, homemaker, and mother. Her sampler was almost like a JDate profile. It included careful stitching of her name, age, the alphabet, and the date the sampler was finished. Prospective suitors would admire the craftsmanship and sentiments of the sampler in the same way a young man might look at a girl's online profile photo today. It's interesting that the unremarkable, mostly unrecorded lives of these young colonial women live on in these lovely handmade projects.

Self-reliance is the cornerstone of independence and a key component of personal happiness. A measure of self-reliance and creativity is the ability to "make it yourself." Learn how to bake bread. The smell of a homemade loaf coming out of the oven will fill your home and your heart with pride. Bake a pie. A woman's culinary ability has always been closely linked with her desirability as a wife. "Can she bake a cherry pie, Billy boy, Billy boy?" And it is the very proud husband who boasts, "She can make a cherry pie, quick as a cat can wink an eye." You don't know how to bake? Read a cookbook! If you can read, you can bake—and cook.

It's especially satisfying to make something unexpected—things that are almost always store-bought. I make pickles. Everybody loves pickles and is amazed when you say that you made them yourself. They are as easy to make as putting small cucumbers or other vegetables in a jar to marinate for weeks in a brine of lots of salt, sugar, vinegar, water, and whatever herbs and spices you like. The hardest part of making pickles is remembering to put up a jar of them weeks before you want to serve them.

I frequently entertain classmates and love to have my school colors on the table. Always a huge hit are orange and black truffles. Melt a bag of bittersweet chocolate chips, add a softened bar of cream cheese, three cups of confectioners' sugar, and a little boozy flavoring like rum or amaretto. Mix it well, refrigerate for an hour, and then roll walnut-size balls in powdered cocoa, chopped nuts, flaked coconut, or my favorite . . . orange and black nonpareils!

Okay, maybe you just don't love being in the kitchen. Learn to knit. Did you know that Mr. Rogers's mother crafted every sweater he wore on his popular children's television program? Maybe you could crochet a doily. Or sew a patchwork quilt. You don't know how to do needlework? Again, read a book. You'll surprise yourself. Using your head *and* your hands will satisfy a special place in your heart. Do you remember the joy you experienced in second grade when you gave your mother the wooden cigar box covered with macaroni and spray-painted gold and proudly said, "I made this for you all by myself"? The pride of craftsmanship stays with you. My mother still has this jewelry box.

I've advanced beyond pasta creations into beadwork, weaving tiny beads in intricate patterns around plastic Easter eggs. The devil doesn't really make work for idle hands, but it is heavenly to create something beautiful with your own hands.

Sometimes the greatest happiness can be found in the simplest things that we do for ourselves and for the ones we love. As a young person, you'll naturally want to explore and experiment broadly. That's how we learn and grow. But after countless fancy meals in expensive restaurants, you'll come to appreciate the simple, home-cooked meal. And even the most social-climbing, jet-setting A-listers reach a point where they long for the quiet night spent at home. By the end of *Candide*, the characters have traveled the world, acquired great fortunes, and suffered tremendous hardships before they find the secret to true happiness. "We build our home, and chop our wood, and make our garden grow."

Smart Advice

- The more you do for yourself, the more empowered you'll feel.
- Self-reliance is the cornerstone of independence.
- What you create tells the world who you are. Create something delicious. Create something beautiful.

Get All the Questions Right

$\mathcal{H}$E LOVES ME; HE LOVES ME NOT. WHETHER THE OBJECT OF YOUR AF-
fection is actually sweet on you has nothing to do with which sentiment
you express while plucking the last petal from the daisy. Frankly, if you
are resorting to botanical soothsaying, your relationship is probably not
on very solid ground.

Almost never are there any tricks, rituals, or magic involved in
achieving your life's goals. You have to be methodical in how you plan
for your personal happiness and remain focused on what you want and
how you are going to get it. As with all things, luck can play a part, but
more often than not . . . you make your own luck. Both personally and
professionally, you have to plan your work and then work your plan.
Don't leave your happiness to chance, and don't be afraid to move forward, even if it requires your first taking a step back. The path to happiness and success is rarely a straight line.

Are you wondering whether he is the one? You probably already
know whether he truly cares for you, and you almost certainly know
whether you deeply care for him. Of course, some relationships bloom

over time, and others wither. Some do both, repeatedly. Relationships aren't static, and you'll probably reevaluate and course-correct many times during their evolution. The best marriages are the ones that can sustain the vicissitudes of fortune and misfortune that life always brings. Because relationships are defined by an ever-changing dynamic, the best you can do at any point is the *best you can do* with what you have and what you know.

If you're in your late teens or early twenties, and dating a man who is neither good to you nor good for you, get out of the relationship and find a better man. If you've already invested a few years with him, it's hard to admit defeat, extricate yourself, and get back in the dating market, but do so sooner rather than later. Are you hanging in there in the hopes that you can show him how to be a better man? You can't and he won't, and if you wait too long to end things, your dating options will diminish . . . rapidly. Sometimes you have to cut your losses and run. How do you know that you'll find a better man? You don't know for sure, but if the man you're with is already making you unhappy, he'll probably continue to do so. Move on. Leaving a bad situation is no real *loss* to you—it's an *opportunity* for a new start with a better partner. Afford yourself the time to explore other options while you are still an object of desire, because the bloom will be off that rose much sooner than you think.

How happy should you expect to be in a relationship? It depends on what you think a happy relationship looks like. Most young people use their parents' marriage as the standard by which they judge coupled bliss. If your parents had a troubled partnership, the bar you set may be very low—or it may propel you to set that bar at unreasonable heights. The truth is that in evaluating your personal situation, you have to filter out the static coming at you from outside sources, and ultimately trust your instincts. Your friends mean well, but they aren't living in your platform pumps. Only you know whether the pain of being *with* him is greater or less than the pain of being *without* him. Joy isn't a reliable measure of happiness in a relationship, because it is blinding. Pain is a better gauge—it's sobering and somehow more tangible and quantifiable than joy. At any given time, if you listen to your inner self, you know everything that can be known about how you feel and what you need. The answer lies neither in the stars nor the flowers. You know what you have to do. Just do it!

When my sons were of the age when standardized tests loom very large for students, I marveled at the lengths to which other families would go to ensure the best test-taking outcome for their children. For months before the SATs, there were weekend prep classes, private tutors, and expensive study software. Days before, there would be the purchase of a dozen new No. 2 pencils, erasers, and new batteries for new calculators. The night before the exam there was a high-protein dinner, and the morning of the test, their kids sat down to a power breakfast, before the car service arrived to take them to the test site. As they walked out the door, the parents reminded them of all the special tips they'd picked up on how to take tests. What these parents didn't do was instill in their children the value of learning, or the discipline to be devoted students. Doing well on standardized tests (or in life) depends on focus, commitment, and dedication—not tricks and gimmicks. When my boys would walk out the door to take the subway to the test site, the only advice I would offer was "Get all the questions right." That's all they had to do—and mostly, they did. And so should you.

In my family, *Get all the questions right* has become shorthand for ". . . you know everything that can be known at this time; you know what you have to do; do it!" Whether you are taking an exam, the score of which can significantly impact your educational options, or evaluating whether the relationship you are in is the one that you want to keep for a lifetime, don't be guided by parlor games like the Decision of the Flower. Do the work, because there are very few shortcuts to success. These are the most important endeavors and decisions you'll ever undertake. Think deeply. Listen to your inner self and get all the questions right.

Smart Advice

- You know everything that can be known at this time.
- You know what you have to do.
- Do it!

The Gender Equality Fallacy

*W*HY IS MY ADVICE DIRECTED ONLY TOWARD WOMEN? BECAUSE MEN don't need advice on dating and marriage. They can take their whole lives to get married and start families. As a woman who dreams of marriage and motherhood, you must be very cognizant of the fact that time is not on your side. You have a limited number of years after college to find THE ONE and then an even more limited number of years to start a family before yours is considered a high-risk pregnancy. Men don't need to be reminded of anything—other than how lucky they are to have such a huge window of opportunity within which to marry and have children. And men of the Ivy League? Fuggetaboutit! Their desirability increases every year after they graduate, until they are no longer on solid food. Sorry, girls, the truth is that women's desirability peaks in their twenties, and then plummets off the cliff, so you have to seriously plan for your personal happiness with purpose and dedication.

The fact is, men and women are not the same. Don't believe anyone who tells you different.

Their bodies and brains are different and function in ways that define their gender. Men are physically bigger and stronger. Their body parts are external, and designed for the quick deposit and retreat. Women's bodies are the nests that nurture and nourish. Beyond physical comparisons, some thought processes and instinctive capabilities are distinct to each gender. For instance, women are better at finding things and remembering where things are. I recently read that it is because females instinctively navigate by using landmarks, whereas males are more prone to rely on cardinal direction, or celestial navigation. There's a reason why husbands are always asking their wives, and sons are always asking their mothers, where stuff is. It's not because the uterus is a tracking device; it is because women are hardwired for locating things.

Despite these many differences, of course, men and women *should* be afforded equal rights, equal pay, and equal opportunities. However, the biological limitations on a woman's childbearing years invalidate any declaration of gender equality. Men can take a lifetime to find a wife and begin a family. Women just don't have that kind of time.

A ticking biological clock makes all the difference and will always be an impediment to true gender equality.

Yes, I understand that the quality of sperm diminishes with age. Studies show that from ages fifty to eighty, male sperm count is only 75 percent that of younger men. But do you know how many of the little swimmers we're talking about? Men produce between 40 million and 500 million sperm . . . in a good ejaculation. And then they just produce more of it . . . and they can do so every day. So even at 75 percent, they are producing between 30 million and 375 million sperm per day. It is estimated that in their lifetime, men produce around 7,500,000,000,000 sperm. I don't think I even know the name for a number with this many zeroes. Gazillion?

Women are born with *all* of our eggs in two ovarian baskets—

around 400 mature eggs during our reproductive lifetime. So, let's compare the numbers . . . 7,500,000,000,000 versus 400. I spent my college years as an art history major, and never even took a math course, but even I can analyze this equation . . .

NOT EQUAL!

Think about it . . . that we are even *talking* about the sperm count of eighty-year-old men! We are clearly *not* considering the conception rates of women in their eighties, or seventies, or sixties, or fifties. And when women become pregnant in their mid-forties, it's common to look for a star to rise in the east.

Everyone enters into the possibility of parenthood in their teen years. Men continue to produce sperm for forty years after women are left with powdered eggs. Again, I'm neither a scientist nor a mathematician, but a twenty-five-year window of opportunity to bear children versus almost seventy years of possible baby making . . .

NOT EQUAL!

When a baby is conceived and delivered, the contributor of the egg and the winning sperm are equally called mother and father. However, a woman will solely bear the responsibility of nine months of gestation, morning sickness, swollen ankles (swollen everything, really), hours of excruciating labor, the trauma of delivery, and postpartum symptoms, and work for months to regain her figure. Men have a twenty-second sperm contribution.

NOT EQUAL!

I hope that parents tell their sons that if a girl that they have been intimate with becomes pregnant, they have to act responsibly. That is fair and reasonable, and it's what a *man* does. However, I hope that parents are telling their *daughters* that they are *solely* responsible for their own bodies. Regardless of whether a man says that he is taking precautions, it is a woman's body that will carry a child and ultimately it is a woman's responsibility to ensure that appropriate birth control measures are taken. And if an unwanted pregnancy occurs, the man may come to the hospital or clinic, he may be sympathetic and comforting, and he may pay for the procedure, but it is the woman alone who will suffer the physical and emotional trauma of an unborn child being removed from her body.

NOT EQUAL!

Beyond the physical challenges of pregnancy, if men and women equally aspire to parenthood, the limitations on a woman's time frame to bear children place extraordinary pressure on her to procreate before it's too late. The stress of a loudly ticking biological clock is an added burden that men—with their seventy-year window of opportunity—don't even consider.

We all know men in their fifties and sixties who are married to women twenty or thirty years their junior—with toddlers at home. They frequently have two families. These men have grown children by their first wives and babies with their new wives. They divorced in their late forties, remarried in their fifties, and here they are pushing strollers to preschool and swings at the park. At the local playgrounds, they are regularly assumed to be the children's grandfathers. Some actually have grandchildren older than their own children by their second (or third) wives. Women don't have two families, because they don't have the same window of opportunity to bear children that men do.

Charlie Chaplin was seventy-four when his youngest was born.

Cary Grant was sixty-two when his only child was born.

South Carolina governor and senator Strom Thurmond's first (legitimate) child was born when he was sixty-eight. His last child was born when he was seventy-four.

Author Saul Bellow's last child was born when he was eighty-four years old.

Funnyman Steve Martin became a first-time father at age sixty-seven. I don't know who Mrs. Steve Martin is, but I'm pretty sure she's not sixty-seven.

We can agree that neither gender is intrinsically better or more worthy than the other. But being equal in worth, or value, is not the same as being identical or interchangeable. Beyond testosterone and estrogen, body parts and natural instincts, men and women are just different.

Smart Advice

- Remember that men and women are not the same physically, psychologically, or emotionally.
- Men can take their whole lives to marry and have children. Women can't. Don't waste time, girls.
- Birth control is ultimately a woman's responsibility because it is only a woman's body that will carry a child.

Life/Work Balance

*W*ORK/LIFE BALANCE? IT SHOULD REALLY BE LIFE/WORK BALANCE.

Your life is more important than your work, and you should put the most important stuff first.

It is said that on one's deathbed, nobody regrets not having spent more time at the office. That's probably not true. Some people live to work. They wake up in the morning and go to sleep at night thinking about little more than their jobs: how they can further distinguish themselves in their workplace, navigate that tricky corporate terrain more effectively, get promoted faster, earn more money. They are probably very good at what they do, and when they die, their memorial service will likely be packed with professional colleagues who will come to pay their respects. However, during his or her lifetime, the dearly departed probably came home to an empty apartment.

That doesn't seem like a life well spent, unless that's the life you choose. But why would you choose a one-dimensional existence? Of course, combining career and family is challenging, but it's certainly doable. Men have been doing it forever—they went to work while the little lady cared for home and family. The rare man who never took that trip down the aisle—the carefree bachelor—was probably more pitied than envied, unless he was very wealthy, in which case he likely didn't want for the companionship of women. Today, even the most (especially the most) accomplished men manage to also be husbands and fathers. In fact, their professional success was probably hastened and enabled by the support of a loving family. Women can do the same—it's just harder.

Why is it harder? It's harder because only women have the babies. For everything else that changes in the gender equality equation, the new world order and the cosmic realignment of the sexes, it's only the women who have the babies. Modernized maternity-leave policies don't controvert this physiological fact. The uncomfortable months leading up to delivery as well as postpartum recovery are not equally shared with even the best-intentioned dad. And through infancy, babyhood, and toddler years, it is mom who is primarily drawn to children when they are in need. And not *just* when they are in need—there must also be some biological imperative that makes most women *want* to be with their babies. Embrace that, because in the context of a long life, your children are with you only for a very short time. If you are a new mom, your days of feeding baby and changing diapers may seem long and the tedium can feel interminable, but ask any mom of grown children and she will tell you how quickly those days pass. And ask any mom of grown children who also has a spectacular career, and she will probably tell you that for all of her professional success, her greatest accomplishment— what she is most proud of—is her children.

The joy and value of caring for your babies can't be overstated. Unless you invent something extraordinary, or otherwise distinguish yourself in some noteworthy, newsworthy profession, it is your children that will be your legacy—the thing that you will be remembered by. So when you consider how to dedicate the lion's share of your time and efforts, think about where that contribution will be most meaningful—invested in preparing another quarterly earnings report, or caring for your babies in their formative years. Being a stay-at-home mom may not be right for everyone, but if it's right for you, don't let anyone minimize your choice. The extreme progressives often refer to parenting as caretaking. Instead of embracing motherhood as the sacred role it is, they diminish it by using a term that is more akin to a groundskeeper or a custodian than it is to a loving mother.

Reentry into the workforce after a leave of absence happens all the time. The ease (or difficulty) with which you can rejoin the working world will vary depending on the field or industry you work in and how long a leave you take. You can recover lost time on the job—but not in your children's lives. For most parents, we have eighteen years from the time they are born until they leave for college. Of course, those are the same eighteen years when you could be making great strides professionally, but if your occupation doesn't lend itself to working from home, then you can't be both on the job and with your kids. When your children are launched, the workforce will still be there for you to reenter. When your job ends, you are downsized, or you retire, your kids will probably be long gone. If you have nothing but your work, then that's what will define you. You might genuinely love your job, but in all likelihood, unless it is your own business or you are in an age-proof industry, it will eventually end.

I work with accomplished, professional women all the time who delay marriage and motherhood because they think that planning a wedding, going on a honeymoon, or taking maternity leave would be a serious intrusion on their work life.

Well, yes . . . there is an inherent inconvenience to marriage and motherhood, just as there is in taking a vacation. They require serious scheduling, they disrupt the otherwise normal course of your life, and they could have the effect of slowing down your meteoric rise in the workplace.

I have one client who refers to her three-year-old daughter as her "little speed bump."

Of course, husbands and fathers don't usually experience those maternity leave setbacks, but moms certainly do. Instead of thinking about these life events as slowing you down, think of them as changing your life, because they do. Yes, there is never a *convenient* time to get married, take vacation, change jobs, or have a baby. But these things are the stuff of our dreams, the things we'll always remember and be remembered by—and for many women, their greatest joys. Work will wait.

Smart Advice

- You have a big life in front of you. Work is only a (small) part of it.
- There is never a convenient time to get married or have a baby. Don't delay.
- Marriage and motherhood aren't inconveniences; they are life's greatest joys.

Fear of Failure

$\mathcal{Y}$OU HAVE TO EVENTUALLY PUT YOUR ROWBOAT IN THE WATER. I know . . . you're practically immobilized by the thought that you might choose the wrong body of water in which to launch your boat, and set off paddling in the wrong direction. Don't worry so much about how to begin. It doesn't really matter where you start, because most water is connected to other water. Take the plunge and start paddling— if you're not happy with the direction in which your boat or your life is going, change course. Life is filled with course corrections. Don't be so afraid of making a poor choice that you don't make *any* choice. The sooner you start testing the waters, the sooner you'll be smoothly sailing to your safe, satisfying harbor. And you might be surprised by where the journey takes you. Be open-minded; it might take to you the most unexpectedly wonderful place.

As a very young person, your possible paths to happiness are almost endless, as are your opportunities to recalibrate and redirect your efforts if you misstep or change your mind. You don't have very much, so what do you have to lose? Roll the dice! You might get lucky early and find yourself sitting on top of the world you imagined, or a brilliantly satisfying place that you could never have imagined. If you don't realize your dream early, it will take more time, effort, energy, and perseverance, and the grit to keep going. Believe in yourself and the fact that you'll get there. The roughest patches you encounter are often the ones from which you'll have learned the most, and in retrospect will likely make for the best stories that you'll ever tell your own children!

We all take calculated risks—all the time. We make the best decisions that we can make, with the information that is available to us at the time that we have to decide: which career path to choose, which job to take, which man to marry. Don't be so afraid of not making the right choice, because the truth is that in most circumstances there is *more* than one right choice. Smart, talented, industrious people will succeed in almost any industry and can master almost any job function. And with every professional position they hold, they learn more about where their passions truly lie and what sort of work environment they are best suited to.

When marveling at the unexpected pairing of certain couples, or the likelihood of an unmarried person eventually finding a spouse, my mother used to say, "Every pot has a cover." In fact, most pots have *more* than one cover. It's important to remember this plurality. If you believe that there is only one true love of your life, the pressure on you to find this one and only person will be overwhelming and that can seriously derail your life plan for happiness. Planning for your personal success is very similar to planning for your professional success: you establish some basic criteria—core competencies, common goals, acceptable geography—and then you hope for the best and prepare to course-correct if necessary. When you are conducting a job search, many companies and positions could probably be very satisfying choices for you. Don't think that there is only one right job or right employer. Pick a good company, distinguish yourself by your conscientious work, pay attention to the functions performed by others around you, and keep an eye on emerging opportunities within and outside of your workplace.

When searching for a life partner, if you start with a pool of candidates who share your record of achievement, your core values, and your background, there are probably many men who could be very good husband choices. Women who don't understand that there is more than one good choice to make often waste a lifetime waiting for the one and only Mr. Right and wind up alone. There were probably many men whom these women passed over for reasons of indecision, or fear of making the wrong decision, or the belief that someone better is out there. There may not be, and women simply can't wait too long to marry if they want to bear their own children in a traditional marriage. Look for the best man who shares your core values, and trust that if he believes what you believe, together you'll find your personal path to happiness. Start looking early and keep present in your thoughts the realities of your fertility limitations. Sometimes it isn't practical to hold out for each nuance you ever hoped for in a man. Does he *really* have to be taller than you? Is it *imperative* that he likes foreign films and French food? Probably not. Be realistic in your expectations and demands. By holding out for everything, you may end up with nothing.

A huge component of happiness on the job and happiness in marriage is the sheer determination to make it work. Whatever decision you make about which job offer to accept or whom to marry *becomes* the right choice when you commit yourself to *making* it the right choice. Assuming that you've chosen a company of integrity, they have as much invested in ensuring your successful work experience as you do in having a positive professional experience with them. Their reputation is enhanced or damaged by what employees say about them, just as your future job references are contingent upon their being happy with your performance. Don't be afraid of failing. Do your best. Your employer wants you to succeed as much as you do. Most any job can be the right job if you commit yourself to doing it well.

You'll know that you found the right man when it's clear by his words and actions that he is as committed to making your relationship succeed as you are. Ultimately, men value the comfort of a happy, committed relationship as much as women do. Despite the astronomical divorce rate, go into your marriage with the expectation of success—until death do you part.

Smart Advice

- Roll the dice! Take a chance. You might get lucky.
- Be realistic in your expectations of potential husbands.
- By holding out for everything, you may end up with nothing.
- Commit yourself to making *your* choice the *right* choice.

Take It Back!

SOMEWHERE ALONG THE WAY, MANY YOUNG WOMEN GAVE AWAY their dream of finding a husband and starting a family, in exchange for a life on the job and the safety of a mob. The mob, of course is composed of the virulent feminists and extreme progressives who would have these girls believe that they are too independent to want a man, that work matters more than family, and that there is something *wrong* with the pursuit of marriage and motherhood. Wait a minute . . . why would you give that away? Take it back!

Aren't you tired of being told what you should and should not want? The endless preaching about breaking through glass ceilings and having it all is laced with an unspoken disapproval of your desire to pursue a traditional path to happiness, if that's what you want. Take back your right to choose the life that you want for yourself! You are an adult, and are entitled to want what *you* want without the approval of anyone or any group. Don't feel like you must go with the flow lest you be the object of scorn or ridicule by feminists. Why would you even care about the disapproval of these women? You probably don't like them on any level, but truthfully, you have nothing to fear from them. Yes, they are a very vocal and vitriolic bunch, but if you hold fast to what you want, they can't hurt you. Remember that they're not hurling sticks and stones. It should be pretty clear that these nasty loudmouths are the bitter remnants of the once-proud women's movement whose mission was to empower women to pursue *all* that they want for themselves. Instead, these girls are all about empowering the *cause* . . . not you. Don't allow them to do so at your expense.

You know better than to think that you should abandon your beliefs in favor of the ideas of this disgruntled bunch. They are like the self-serving weavers in a modern-day tale of the Emperor's New Clothes, who would have you believe that you don't need a man, don't want a man, and that going it alone is somehow noble. The same fear and intellectual vanity that led townspeople to admire the naked emperor may be propelling you to adopt a perspective that simply isn't authentic to who you are. If what you want is to climb the corporate ladder and become a titan of industry, then go for it. But if what you *really* want is to be married and have children, then you have to reclaim your right to pursue that goal with complete steadfastness. Get your head in the game and don't wind up parading through town, naked . . . and alone.

In quiet, contemplative moments, when you think deeply about who you are and the life you hope to lead, it is probably inclusive of meaningful work *and* a loving family, yes? But honestly, where are your priorities? Do you imagine the pinnacle of your life to be in a corporate setting or on the arm of your loving husband on the occasion of your children's college graduation or wedding day? If above all you want to be a CEO for a VC or B2B or a NASDAQ or Fortune 500 company then keep listening to the feminist rhetoric that will keep you at a distance from the men you want in your life. But if a loving *family* defines your dream for personal happiness, *stop lying to yourself* and take back your right to choose the path that's right for you, regardless of what other young women are doing.

Speaking of what's fashionable among your girlfriends, do you *really* want to engage in hookups and uncommitted sex? It's certainly available to you if that's what you want, but think about whether you are doing so because all of your friends are, or because it's what young men expect of you. Neither is a good reason. If you choose to have casual sex to satisfy your *own* appetite, well . . . that's your decision. But do so safely and be discreet.

Regardless of how progressive we've become in our attitudes toward sex, physical intimacy is a private thing. What you do and with whom you do it is *very* personal and should neither be bragged about, complained about, or even shared—except perhaps with your most trusted friend. When young men smugly tout their conquests in locker rooms, it is repugnant. When women do so, it's even worse—it's undignified and can harm their reputation indefinitely. Forty years after we were first students at Princeton, my classmates still remember the girls who were promiscuous on campus. Most of them got married, had children, and distinguished themselves in science, medicine, business, and government—but when their names are mentioned, it is still with a knowing snicker.

If, despite your better judgment, you've engaged in casual relationships because you felt like it was the thing to do—just stop doing it. Obviously, virginity isn't a bell that you can unring, but there is no need to keep up a pretense or practice to satisfy anyone's expectations but your own. Choose for yourself whether this is what *you* want in a relationship. If it isn't . . . walk away and look for something more meaningful.

There are plenty of times in a lifetime when circumstances leave us feeling helpless or even victimized. The nonsmoker who is diagnosed with lung cancer, the twenty-eight-year-old bride who is told that she can't conceive a child, or the woman who experiences miscarriage after miscarriage—they had neither responsibility for their misfortunes nor any choice in the matter. You *have* options in how you choose to conduct your life and in what dreams you choose to pursue.

Don't allow the agenda of anyone or any group to supplant the choices that you want for yourself. You have the power to make these decisions that will define the arc of your life.

Don't give that power away. If you already have . . . take it back!

Smart Advice

- Choose the life that you want for yourself, regardless of what other young women are doing.
- Satisfy your own expectations, not those of others.
- If you've stopped listening to your inner self and abandoned control of your life, change course and take it back!

What You Heard Is Not What I Said

*T*HERE ARE FEW THINGS THAT ARE A BETTER INDICATOR OF A GOOD relationship than the ability of two people to communicate with each other clearly and honestly. It requires finesse to tell someone you care about that they have hurt your feelings or that their new habit of telling off-color jokes is making you uncomfortable. Likewise, it sometimes requires acute listening skills and perception to understand that when your *amour du jour* says that he doesn't like your friends, maybe what he means is that he feels left out when you're with them. Or maybe he really doesn't like your friends. Either way, all successful relationships (romantic, professional, or friendly) require the effective exchange of ideas. If you're not sure of what you're being told, ask for clarification. If it's still not clear, ask that it be repeated in other words. Don't walk away from an important conversation without certainty that you understand what you were told and that you were clearly understood.

Every now and again, something is said—or rather, something is *heard* that sets off a chain reaction, often resulting in seismic relationship shifts and hurt feelings. Before you get all bent out of shape, think carefully about the possibility either that you misheard or that what was said wasn't meant as an offense.

When I was a sophomore, I took a philosophy course with a classmate who roomed with two other classmates whom I knew quite well. I didn't really know him, but we were in lectures together and before the midterm exam he asked whether we should get together one night to study for the test. It sounded like a good idea, so I went to his room. He was a junior and had a larger and more comfortable room than mine. He was lying on the carpeted floor poring over the textbook when I arrived. I settled into a beanbag chair next to him and had started paging through my notes when he reached over to flip on the stereo. He put on a Sonny & Cher record and said, "All this is good for is back-rubbing."

Hmm . . . this struck me as less subtle than I might have expected, but it was harmless foreplay that was very common on campus and it was a welcome distraction from studying philosophy. So I got down on the floor and began rubbing his back. After a few minutes, he turned around and attempted to pull me closer to him for a kiss. Well, this certainly wasn't what I signed up for! Self-righteous and offended, I took my notebook and left in a huff. It wasn't until several days later that I ran into one of his roommates, who asked me about what happened the night I was in his room studying. I didn't know what to say. He went on. "Dave said that you were over studying, and he put on some music that he said was 'Only good for back*ground . . .*' "

Take a minute to let that sink in. Clearly, what I heard is not what Dave said.

I suppose that I come by my proclivity for the presumptive insult honestly. When my parents came to America in 1949, their first apartment was a walk-up on the Lower East Side of Manhattan. I'm sure that it was appointed beautifully, thanks to my mother's creativity and excellent sewing skills. All of the Eastern European survivors came to New York within a few years of each other, but the ones who arrived the soonest were first to become acquainted with American customs, nuances, and idioms. My parents were on the latter end of this wave of immigration. There was an occasion when some of the more assimilated friends came to visit my parents' home and, admiring the lovely curtains and bed linens, attempted to compliment my mother by saying, "Estucia, your apartment is so beautiful, it should be on Fifth Avenue!" My mother, not understanding it to be the most luxurious street in New York City, but very aware of the mathematical concept of ordinal numbers as a ranking tool, was deeply offended and shot back with "Fifth Avenue? Why not *First* Avenue?"

Of course, there are occasions when the insult you hear is indeed the insult that was intended. And there are times that you may not even know that you've been insulted until long after the insulter has exited. Groucho Marx famously left a boring party saying, "I've had a perfectly wonderful evening . . . but this wasn't it."

If something you hear just doesn't sound right, ask for clarification until it makes sense to you. Rather than assume the worst, be sure that you understand the words and the meaning, lest you find yourself as Mel Brooks's 2000 Year Old Man slapping his face in both hands at the realization that what he perceived as Paul Revere's anti-Semitism, "The Yiddish are coming, the Yiddish are coming!" was maybe intended as something else.

Miscommunications are not limited to verbal exchanges. They can also happen in print. A political activist may understand the word *unionized* to mean belonging to a labor union, but the more scientifically inclined might see the same word as referring to the reversal of a conversion of something into ions. If you're not certain of definition or intention . . . ask!

Any communication that requires interpretation or translation from one language to another necessitates special attention. There is an urban legend involving General Motors' confusion over their failed introduction of the Chevy Nova automobile in South America. Native speakers translated *nova* as "does not go," hardly a winning moniker for a vehicle. Likewise, saying *estoy embarazada* does *not* mean "I am embarrassed" in Spanish; it means "I am pregnant." If you're not sure of the linguistic precision of a language with which you are only moderately familiar . . . stick with your native tongue. It's better to be accurately understood as a single-language speaker than to be thought of as a misinformed polyglot who is expecting a bouncing baby blunder!

Sometimes when dealing with people who speak foreign languages, it's more important to intuit what they are trying to say than to parse every word. Many years ago I worked intensely with a Norwegian entrepreneur who was establishing an American presence for a business he had founded in Scandinavia. It was a point-of-purchase advertising medium that was directly connected with the petroleum industry. I hired domestic staff for him as well as conducted industrial research and worked on a variety of other special projects for him as needed. He knew I was conscientious, detail-oriented, and extremely tenacious. He came to rely on me for many things and frequently would say, in his thick Norwegian accent, things like "Susan, I would like you to *overlook* the particulars of the upcoming sales meeting in Houston." He didn't mean that he wanted me to ignore or disregard those details. He meant *oversee*, not overlook. If English weren't one's primary language, it would be easy enough to confuse those two words. There are occasions when you simply have to *listen* with an accent.

Smart Advice

- All successful relationships require effective communication.
- If you're not sure of what you heard, ask for clarification until you do.
- Be sure that you are clearly understood by others.

Watch Your Mouth!

*P*ERHAPS IT'S BECAUSE I'VE BEEN AN HR BABE FOR DECADES, BUT AN odd bit of career advancement advice has always stuck with me: Dress for the job you want, not the job you have.

I've made that recommendation many times to young people who aspired to corporate management but continued to dress like interns. Your sartorial presentation sets a mental image of you in the minds of people who may be instrumental in deciding whether a promotion goes to the woman who wears conservative clothes and low pumps, or to you in your tank top and flip-flops. Again, as an experienced HR professional I know that in all likelihood, the promotion goes to the gal who looks corporate, responsible, and mature. Businesses promote people who put forward an image that is consistent with their corporate identity, so consider your outfit choices carefully before you head to the office.

In the same way that your wardrobe can help or hurt you on the job, so can your language mark you favorably or unfavorably. Using trashy, vulgar, obscene, or blasphemous words in the workplace is a mistake. Regardless of how stressful a job may be, the use of bad English is usually interpreted as a lack of professionalism, self-control, and maturity; it can be the difference between being taken seriously as a professional and being disregarded. As Professor Higgins said to Colonel Pickering of Eliza Doolittle, "If you spoke as she does, sir, instead of the way you do, why you might be selling flowers, too!"

Be mindful of the words you use. Think of the careers that have been marred by inappropriate language: Don Imus, George "Macaca" Allen, Michael Richards (*Seinfeld*'s "Kramer"), to name a few. Social media has made it virtually impossible to escape a slip of the tongue. You might get away with an indiscretion, but don't count on it. Just when you think that nobody is listening to you, or that only your brother and a few close friends read your blog, the obscene thing that you said or wrote goes viral. Image management used to be the exclusive purview of the rich and famous; the Internet has now made it everyone's concern.

Auditory memory can be as powerful and as potentially damaging as visual memory. Before you let loose a string of obscene invectives, think about whether you want to be remembered for and defined by your constant profanity. It's not at all attractive—not in truck drivers, and certainly not in you. It's entirely possible that your vulgar language will not only turn off employers, but also be off-putting to potential suitors as well. Young men think wistfully about the girl they will someday marry. It is very possible that when they hear your obscenities and vulgarities, they will ponder the fact that that is the same mouth you will use to kiss your (and his) babies.

The lady you are in word, deed, and dress reflects on the man you're with and the life he hopes to live. Put forward a consistent image of being gracious, lovely, and ladylike, just as you want your future husband to be seen as an eloquent, mannerly gentleman. And the admirable language that parents use in the home is remembered and mimicked by their children.

Excessive profanity can make anyone look inelegant, classless, and stupid—as if they simply don't have the language skills necessary to express himself or herself convincingly without cursing. Some of the most respected comedians, such as Jerry Seinfeld and Bill Cosby, don't work *blue*, because they understand that if comics have to resort to invoking curse words, then they probably haven't nailed the joke—they are instead just going for the cheap laugh. Verbal eloquence is sophisticated and reflects good taste and judgment; the habitual use of expletives is a coarse and undesirable trait that can label you as a careless person, lacking in creativity, dignity, and intelligence.

Of course, there is a time and a place for profanity. Some of the most brilliant people I know regularly pepper their conversation with swearing for effect, but they only do so in *very* select company and only *after* it is absolutely clear to everyone within earshot that they are capable of elegant, scholarly discourse. Dropping the F-bomb takes no talent and demonstrates no cleverness—it is usually nothing more than a gratuitous gambit for immediate attention. You can do better than that.

Directness is admirable, but it's not always wise for whatever is on your mind to be on your tongue. Be judicious in what you share publicly and privately—if it is offensive, it reflects badly on you and could make others uncomfortable. As a rule, find something more appropriate to discuss than bathroom humor, sex, or tirades against religion or people of faith. This verbal pollution is damaging on so many levels. Cursing a blue streak becomes tedious much faster than you might think. Don't think of this suggestion as a curtailment of your freedom of speech, but instead as a return to decency. Rejecting profanity is neither backward nor prudish; it is a call for a better, smarter type of communication. In the absence of a swear jar, listen to your own speech patterns and be cognizant of whether you are falling into the habit of using expletives out of sheer laziness. It's an easy habit to pick up, and for those who do, profanity becomes second nature. They spew curses with the annoying frequency that teenagers say "like" and "ya know." As a well-educated person, you have a better vocabulary than that. Think about what you're saying and take the few extra seconds to find the *right* words instead of using the wrong ones.

To be as *good* as your word is to suggest that you can be counted on to do as you say you will. Equally true is that you may be seen as being as *bad* as the words you use. Think before you speak—watch your mouth!

Smart Advice

- The lady you are in word and deed reflects on the man you're with. Clean your act up!

- Constant profanity is not attractive in truck drivers, or in you.

- Honestly, is that is the same mouth you will use to kiss your babies?

Kindest Regards

*W*HEN VERY YOUNG WOMEN ARE ASKED ABOUT WHAT THEY LOOK for in a man, their responses reflect their youth: they usually say that they seek a tall man who is handsome, with a great smile, gorgeous hair, and dreamy eyes. Women who are a bit older know better. They look for men who are healthy, stable, and secure and who would be good providers. Mature women know the truth—the most important of *all* qualities in a spouse is kindness. Good looks and financial stability are desirable assets at every life stage, but at the end of the day, the thing that matters most is having a partner who is reliably, consistently, genuinely kind.

Robert Louis Stevenson said, "The essence of love is kindness," but how do you recognize true kindness? It's hard, because everybody attempts to put forward an image of themselves as friendly, generous, and considerate, regardless of whether they actually are. In fact, it is often the most selfish and duplicitous people who try the hardest to look the kindest. Beware of those who regularly regale you with tales of their magnanimity. It's like the egotists who talk too much about how hard they work and how much sex they are having—in actuality, these people are probably not doing much of either. Likewise, true kindness is easily recognized by consistently considerate behavior, and never by self-pronouncement.

Another good measure of genuine kindness is when it is offered unobserved, and without any hope or possibility of getting anything in return. The fellow who extends the same courtesy to the secretary, receptionist, and messenger as he does to the president, CEO, and chairman is a truly kind man. He speaks warmly and with respect to everyone, including those who are virtually invisible to lesser men.

Greater men are attracted to kindness. Think about how *you* treat others around you. The sum of your actions defines your place in the world, and your random acts of kindness could change the lives of others. Many years ago, I was coming home from grocery shopping and as I entered my building, a neighbor and her husband were about to exit the lobby. It was a warm Saturday morning, and to say that I was dressed casually would be an understatement. I came through the revolving doors with my supermarket bags and almost tripped over my neighbor. I glanced up to apologize and noticed that unlike my plain outfit and sneakers, hers was a beautifully tailored damask suit and lovely heels. Her curly brown hair was especially shiny, her makeup was perfect, and she looked radiant, if a bit apprehensive. I knew her well enough to nod and smile when we saw each other in the laundry room but didn't even know her name. But on that morning, I looked at her squarely and told her that she looked absolutely beautiful. She looked at me squarely, smiled from ear to ear, and walked out of the building with her husband.

Months later, we were together in the laundry room and she said that she wanted to thank me for a kindness that I extended to her, which changed her perspective and attitude on one of the most important days of her life. On that warm morning months before, my neighbor and her husband were setting off to attend their son's wedding. She was feeling insecure about how she looked on such a momentous occasion and my unsolicited reassurance was exactly what she needed. She told me that after hearing my sincere compliments, she left our building with confidence and instead of worrying about whether she looked good enough, she thoroughly enjoyed the wedding, and the photographs of the day reflect only her joy. You never know how a small kindness can make a huge difference.

Of course, there is some truth to the adage that no good deed goes unpunished. When my children were in elementary school, I would regularly drop them off in the schoolyard by 8 A.M. and walk back home up York Avenue. One morning I saw a set of keys on the sidewalk between Eighty-Second and Eighty-Third streets. I looked around to see if anyone was rushing down the street looking for lost keys. There was no one. So, I picked them up and noticed that there was an ASPCA tag attached to the key chain. Thinking that I would be a good citizen, I went home and called the ASPCA. I explained that I wanted to return the lost keys and hoped that if I read the numbers off the dog tag, they could give me the address or telephone number of the owner. They could not, but asked for my telephone number so that they could contact the owner, who could then contact me. I gave them my number and hung up feeling virtuous, until the phone rang around a half hour later. An irate woman called me screaming that if I would have just left the keys on the sidewalk she would have found them when she retraced her steps. Because I had picked them up, she thought they were forever lost and she immediately had to go to the expense and inconvenience of having the lock on her apartment changed.

Okay, things don't always work out as we expect they will, but err-

ing on the side of kindness is never really a mistake. In the Jewish tradition we refer to a good deed as a *mitzvah*. Technically, it is more of
a commandment—a holy act that connects heaven and earth—than a
good deed, but *mitzvah* has come to be thought of as synonymous with
an act of kindness. Because Judaism is a religion based more on action
than faith, doing good deeds is central to living a good life.

Everybody, at every life stage and of every station in life, responds
to kindness. Look for it in others, and let the world find it in you. It's a
mitzvah!

Smart Advice

- Genuine kindness is offered unobserved, and without any hope or
  possibility of getting anything in return.
- Everybody responds well to kindness.
- Kindness trumps all.

Bad Childhood? Get Over It!

*Y*OU CAN WALLOW IN YOUR UNFORTUNATE PAST, OR YOU CAN MAKE A conscious choice to rise above it and move forward. I learned many lessons from my mother and father, but none more important than this. They are survivors, and so am I.

My parents were both born in Poland. My mother is a survivor of Auschwitz and my father was liberated from Bergen-Belsen in April 1945. They were married in a displaced persons camp in Germany in 1946 and came to America in the spring of 1949, three months before my brother was born. I followed six years later. They overcame trauma and torture, and came to a new country with a new baby. They didn't speak the language, have family to support them, or have an education that would have afforded many options in this new world. Pop started life in America working in a grocery store on the Lower East Side of Manhattan and he earned twenty-four dollars per week.

Their Eastern European mind-set placed a distinctly different value on sons than on daughters. Sons were everything. My brother was their golden boy, their affirmation of life after near death and unspeakable atrocity. My mother became pregnant while my parents were still in Germany. All of their friends and fellow survivors who came to America in the late 1940s did so by boat to Ellis Island. Passage was free, but was unavailable to women who were more than six months pregnant or had an infant who was less than three months old. My mother was seven months along. They took whatever little money my father earned from working with American troops in the DP camp and purchased two one-way tickets from Frankfort to New York on Pan American Airways. It would be the only time my father was on an airplane.

Why didn't they hold on to their savings, wait six months, and come to America by boat with their baby? I remember asking my mother this and marveling at her response. She told me that she wasn't much of a history student as a girl in Poland, but she did remember that in order to become president, a boy had to be *born* in the United States. My brother didn't pursue a career in government or politics. He was a New York City public school teacher and administrator until his retirement several years ago.

I'm certain that my parents never considered that perhaps *I* aspired to someday become president of the United States. I didn't. However, I certainly wanted something more for myself than the life my parents imagined for me. They just assumed I would marry—ideally, a butcher, so that there would always be meat on the table. As all parents do, mine wanted the best for me. The problem was that they defined what was best for me very differently from how I defined it for myself. Perhaps because their formal education was interrupted by the war, they felt strongly about the importance of a good education . . . for my brother.

My parents didn't expect a daughter to be so challenging, but I was. "Challenging," as in difficult for them to cope with, and challenging as in questioning of their attitudes and choices. As a teenager, I was a very good student and a moderately talented artist. My parents barely saw some practical application for my artistic ability. They thought that if (God forbid) I couldn't find a husband and start a family, maybe I could design greeting cards to earn a few dollars to support myself. Everybody buys greeting cards! What they couldn't see was the value of an advanced education for women and they forbade my pursuing it. It is doubtful that they had ever heard of Princeton when I was considering my post–high school options.

I didn't know how I would overcome the obstacle of my parents' refusal to participate in my college application process. They wouldn't hear of my going away to school and refused to sign any of the necessary documentation. I was warned that if I insisted on pursuing this, I would be doing so without their support, financial or otherwise. From their old-world perspective, to have an unmarried daughter leave their home was a disgrace. Nobody in my family had ever gone away to college. No woman in my family had gone to college at all.

At seventeen years old, I filed my application to Princeton as an emancipated minor, and the rest, as they say . . . is history.

It is often said that adversity builds character. I don't think so. Instead, I would say that adversity *reveals* character. How you stand up and continue to get up off the mat when you've been beaten down shows the world your true colors—and is a reminder of who you are in the world. The strength we gain from misfortune is the knowledge that we survived it.

Don't let your past hold you back or serve as an excuse for why you don't have what you want. Regardless of how many bad experiences you've had, don't allow yourself to continue to be victimized by them. Every new day brings with it the possibility of doing better. Commit to lifting yourself up and moving forward positively.

I've always been inspired by my parents' ability to make a new life for themselves in New York City after World War II. The horrors they endured always stayed with them but never kept them from living their American dream. I dreamed of a different life than theirs, one that was more informed, diverse, creative, and bigger. I dreamed of my future children and how I would parent them differently than I was parented— nurture and encourage them to be everything they wanted to be, regardless of their gender.

Blaming our current failures on past misfortune is unproductive. Dwelling on an unhappy past only perpetuates it. The song goes, "Into each life some rain must fall." It's up to you to pick yourself up, dry yourself off, and get over it!

Smart Advice

- The nobility of victimhood wears thin much quicker than you think.
- Believe that you've been strengthened by your misfortune, and then move on.
- Don't wallow. Be strong. Be smart. Move on!

PART IV

First Find Yourself.
Then Find THE ONE

The way you see yourself and how others (including men) see you is largely a reflection of the way you respond to circumstances and the positions and attitudes to which you are willing to commit. So if you are in serious husband-hunting mode, think deeply about how you deal with things like jealousy, honesty, conformity, tenacity, authenticity, forgiveness, resourcefulness, self-reliance, and reliability.

Finding THE ONE requires you to have first found yourself. Understanding who you are at your core, what drives you, delights you, and infuriates you will go a long way toward knowing the right man when he comes along.

You are the weaver of the tapestry of the life you live. It will define you.

Embroider it richly and authentically.

Speaking Your Truth

$\mathcal{A}$RE YOU BRUTALLY HONEST? HOW MUCH DO YOU VALUE HONESTY IN a relationship? Would you rather be pacified with an untruth than have your feelings hurt? Are you willing to suppress your feelings so as to not risk offending? This is a pretty significant core value, and understanding where you stand on truthfulness can be helpful in knowing whether he is THE ONE. Do you want him to tell you that he's seeing other women, or does what you don't know not hurt you? Most people who play fast and loose with the truth can't be trusted, but they are usually nonconfrontational and thus easy to be with. And the scrupulous truth tellers can be pedantic and prone to oversharing. Think seriously about what the truth means to you and the man you consider marrying.

As I said at the beginning, I am more blunt than most people. For as long as I can remember, I've said what I honestly thought, with few filters and very little concern for whether my heartfelt opinions make others look favorably upon me. Inexplicably, my forthrightness has recently become much more comfortably accepted than it was decades ago. It seems that what is seen as brash in one's twenties is seen as wisdom in one's fifties. My brilliant young son astutely identified this personally transformative phenomenon when he said, "Ma, you've finally grown into your mouth."

Benjamin Franklin was right: Honesty is the best policy. And Robert E. Lee was *more* right when he said, "Honesty is not policy. The real honest man is honest from conviction of what is right, not from policy."

Telling the truth is liberating. *Getting it off your chest* rids you of a burden. It frees up mental real estate and allows you to move forward untrammeled. Sharing your honest opinion feels good, if it is intended for good, and can be tremendously useful to those who might benefit from it. Think about what you know and how you can share it productively. Of course, complete honestly isn't appropriate in all circumstances. Grandma doesn't need to know that you really didn't like the sweater she made you. And telling your friend how much you don't like the new home she just bought or the man she recently married isn't useful. But without compromising your integrity, exercise a little restraint . . . and speak your mind!

I come by my directness honestly. Neither of my parents ever pulled any punches. Whatever was on their minds was on their tongues. After my dad hadn't seen me for a few weeks, it was not uncommon for him to greet me by saying, "What? You've put on some weight? And, you have a pimple on your nose?"

Thanks, Pop. Nice to see you, too.

And while Pop was obviously not well suited for an important position in the diplomatic corps, he was much more tactful than my mother ever was. Several years ago, I recall being with my parents and brother in a small waiting room at Mount Sinai Hospital. I can't recall whether we were there for Ma's normal-pressure hydrocephalus or for Pop's ALS, but we spent a lot of time in this waiting room over many months. One afternoon, there were several other patients waiting, and one more, a morbidly obese woman in a wheelchair, rolled off the nearby elevator and joined the group. My mother looked at her and said (presumably to my dad, brother, and me) in a full voice, "You think I'm fat? Look at that *zatzer!*"* Surely Ma knew that people in wheelchairs aren't deaf, and not knowing the woman, Ma had no cause to openly insult her. I don't know how to explain this other than to say that here is an example of honesty gone amok.

Telling the truth is important. Our truths define us and help us know our place in the world. But how we frame these truths is critical.

When my children were very young, I would tell them that they could say anything to anyone if they kept three things in mind: Be sincere in what you say, be respectful in how you say it, and intend good. Maintaining those three rules, I told my sons that they could speak with their teachers, rabbi, principal, the mayor, or anyone else about anything.

The test of this theory came when my older son was seven years old, in second grade, and came home with another perfect report card—except for his grade in French. The elementary school had a once-a-week language class for the children, taught by an older woman who was described as being impatient and cranky. My sons were always stellar students and took great pride in their superlative report cards, so this less than perfect grade in French was vexing. We talked about it and my son insisted that he did all the homework, did very well on the exams, participated regularly in class, and absolutely deserved a better grade. Although I knew that getting a mediocre mark in a second-grade language class wouldn't be a make-or-break moment in my son's life,

---

* A plopper. A big lump that goes plop! A grossly overweight person.

learning how to stand up for himself honestly, in a positive and productive way, would most certainly stay with him for a lifetime.

We agreed that he (not I) would speak with his teacher. I told him that he had to approach her respectfully and ask if he might speak with her after school, or before class. She was a bit surprised by his request, but agreed to wait for him after school the next day. We talked about how he should be truthful in explaining to her that he felt that he had done all of the work in her class, paid close attention, and contributed to class discussions. He told me that he explained that he took her class seriously as he did all of his classes and put forward his best effort to learn French. He told the teacher that he believed he deserved a better grade than she gave him, and he hoped that she would change his grade. The teacher was surprised that a seven-year-old would care enough to request a meeting. But she understood that he was earnest in his request, and was impressed that he was so respectful in his approach. In reviewing her records, she saw that he was correct in his assertions about his performance, and despite being otherwise impatient and cranky, she was a big enough person and a good enough teacher to upgrade his report card. One of the best ways to inspire and encourage good students (and everyone else) is to recognize sincere efforts and good intentions.

Be honest with yourself and recognize honesty in others. The many reasons for truthfulness are obvious.

And if nothing else, the truth is the easiest thing to remember.

Smart Advice

- Consider whether honesty is the best policy for you.
- Think about your truths and how you can share them productively.
- Our truths define us and help us know our place in the world.

Beware the Green-Eyed Monster

*I*T IS HUMAN NATURE TO COMPARE OURSELVES WITH OUR PEERS. IT'S a touchstone that assures us that we are on track, keeping pace, and where we are supposed to be. Or, it can be the inspiration to step up our game and work a little harder so as not to fall behind in our class.

Okay, your best friend just became engaged to be married, but you remain woefully single with nary a prospect? Okay, she got lucky and found THE ONE. Don't begrudge her happiness. It's counterproductive. Be happy for her, and have faith that if you direct yourself positively and productively, you'll soon be asking her for the number of her photographer, florist, and caterer. Hey, you might even meet someone wonderful at her wedding!

Bette Midler said, "The worst part of success is trying to find someone who is happy for you."

During the happiest periods of your life, and on the occasions of your greatest achievements, expect the scorn of others. Sometimes it will even come from your closest friends, if they haven't achieved what you have. They don't necessarily love you less, but if your success is greater than theirs, it makes them feel like relative failures—and that doesn't sit well with anyone. Their unkindness and catty criticism of you isn't usually about making you feel bad—it's about their trying to make themselves feel better. It's unfortunate how frequently friends will attempt to self-comfort at your expense, but that's human nature. Try to look past it and not let it bother you. In fact, the jealousy of malcontents is a fairly reliable measure of your success. If your detractors are saying truly awful things about you . . . congratulations! You must have achieved greatly to be in such an enviable position. Do your best to ignore those who would malign you; they are usually doing so because you have exceeded their expectations of you—and of themselves.

Most of the time, vicious gossip is a desperate ploy by desperate people who have no better way to distract themselves from their feelings of jealousy. Don't let it get to you. Understand that we are constantly in the process of self-evaluation and that comparing ourselves to our peers is only natural. It's hard to shake off insult—especially public insult—but for your own peace of mind it's usually best not to attempt a counterpunch. Move on.

When I was very young, I thought that jealousy and envy were characteristics of stupid and mean young girls. Most of the great dramas that I can recall from my early school days were created by classmates who were clearly driven by their own jealousy and feelings of insecurity, as well as my own. I had no idea that these emotions and their ugly manifestations span all ages, and in fact get worse with age. There is more at stake. As we mature and acquire greater possessions, position, and wealth, the jealousy of peers is distinctly kicked up a notch, and sometimes masquerades as something else.

Beware of the kind of jealousy that is veiled in the cloak of moral indignation. Instead of directly addressing a difference of opinion, there are those who will attempt to diminish you by claiming to act in the name of some greater good. You'll spot them easily. They are usually the malcontents who live to complain. Much of my advice has been directed to young women who are still students. Some parents of daughters who have already graduated *without* finding husbands have expressed harsh criticism of my advice, claiming that my opinions are insulting to girls who aspire to professional success. Am I saying that their daughters have in any way failed? No, absolutely not. But it's clear by their frustrated parents' misdirected anger that *they* think that their *own* daughters have underperformed, missed an opportunity, or have not lived up to their parents' expectations. There is no "greater good" expressed by these frustrated parents. It must be difficult for them to see the daughters of their friends happily married or engaged, if their own daughters are neither. I suppose that these parents comfort themselves in their moral indignation, but their daughters are probably smart enough to understand the psychodrama being played out in their parents' unreasonable protestations.

We tend to think of jealousy and envy as synonymous. They're not, actually.

Jealousy . . . think of its root, *zeal* or zealously protecting that which you feel anxiety over possibly losing. Envy is wishing you had what others have—and that they didn't have it. They are both destructive emotions, regardless of whether you are the one experiencing them, or are the object of them.

Don't waste your time begrudging others what they have, even if they didn't come by their riches through their own industry. Inherited wealth is still legitimate wealth, and you don't benefit in any way by counting someone else's money. And the girls who are born with naturally thin frames, shining gold hair, and perfect skin came into genetic good fortune honestly. If you didn't, do the best you can with the natural gifts with which you were born. Rather than dwell on the advantages that others were afforded, make sure that you are doing the best that you can do with all that you've got. You probably have more than you think, and your time is much better spent developing your own assets than it is in pointlessly wishing someone else's good fortune was your own.

Just as repugnant as jealousy and envy is reveling in the disappointment of others—especially friends. *Schadenfreude* is a highfalutin German term used to describe feeling delight at someone else's misfortune. It's frequently couched in false sympathy, as in "I'm *so* sorry that you put back on *all* of the weight that you worked so hard to lose." It's sadistic. Be a bigger person than that.

In *Othello*, Shakespeare describes jealousy as a green-eyed monster (not a kitten) for a reason. Jealousy and envy in every form are utterly destructive.

In Yiddish, there is the something known as a *keyn ayn horeh* (pronounced "kin-a-hurrah"). Literally translated as "No to the evil eye," the expression was very common among superstitious grandmothers. It was usually accompanied by their spitting through their fingers three times and looking adoringly at a beloved grandchild. It was spoken to avert the curse of jealousy after something or someone (their perfect grandchild) had been praised.

Say no to the evil eye.

Smart Advice

- Envy is counterproductive and unattractive. Be thankful for your own blessings.

- Celebrate your friends' successes and they'll celebrate yours.

- You don't benefit by counting someone else's money. Play up your own gifts.

Like a Pit Bull on a Pot Roast

*T*ENACITY. DON'T BE SO QUICK TO THROW IN THE TOWEL. HE MIGHT be better than you think. Is it impatience, or our need for immediate gratification that propels us to end relationships before they've had time to develop? Of course, if he treats you poorly, or drinks too much, or doesn't understand any of your cultural references, then maybe this isn't a match made in heaven. But if you share fundamental commonalities (age, marital status, level of education, geographic location, core values), maybe you should look past the more superficial differences and commit yourself to making the relationship work. You can show him the way to dress better, introduce him to a good barber, and even tolerate his Democratic leanings if you are a Republican. None of these things are important. Good men are hard to find and sometimes need a good woman to coax their goodness to the surface. Don't be discouraged. If the basics are in place, stick with him, and the amazing man that he grows into may delight you.

My dog, Lucille, is not a pit bull; she is a dachshund. A sweet, peaceful girl who has much more interest in a nap on the couch than in a walk in the park, she almost never barks, except when the hallway carpet is being vacuumed or the pizza delivery guy is at the door. She is the perfect dog ... until she wants a biscuit. Then she is relentless—whining, begging, closing my computer with her nose, until the biscuit canister is opened and she is given a crunchy treat. No amount of shushing, threatening, begging, or ignoring is effective in thwarting her quest for a biscuit. We should all have this kind of tenacity—especially young people in pursuit of whatever they want for themselves.

When you are a college student, it's sometimes hard to project all of the components that may make up your life's happiness, but there are some elements that you've known for years. You probably know if you want to be married and if you want to have children. This is such an important and personal decision, but peer pressure can persuade you to take your eye off the ball or to redirect your efforts in more politically popular directions. Don't allow yourself to be distracted, or talked away from what you *know* you want.

It comes down to commitment. John Adams famously said, "There are only two creatures of value on the face of the earth: those with the commitment, and those who require the commitment of others." For most young people, the first test of this principle comes in their undergraduate years. Do you enter into a committed partnership, or do you engage into casual, uncommitted relationships? Commitment is hard—it requires intelligence, maturity, and self-possession. Have you picked the right partner, does he share your commitment, could you do better if you took a little longer and looked around more thoroughly? If you're smart, you will have been methodical in your choice, and then it becomes a question of determination to make that choice the *right* choice. Ask any adult who's lived into their fifties or sixties and they will tell you that life can sometimes feel like an endurance test—marriages frequently do. But if you spoke your marriage vows with commitment, then you signed on until death do you part and you figure out how to make it work. This is truly the essence of commitment—doing whatever it takes to overcome obstacles.

In the absence of this kind of determination to make a marriage succeed, partners begin to stray, relationships are easily destroyed, and nobody benefits. Alarming divorce rates testify to a lack of commitment and an unwillingness to work at addressing difficulties and finding a happy balance between two people. Divorce is far from easy, it is in fact excruciating, but it seems to be the preferred response to a marriage that is less than ideal. Don't be so quick to admit defeat if things don't always seem to be going perfectly. Some (most) relationships take time to really hit their stride, and potentially wonderful unions are aborted before they've been given a fair chance and the time to succeed. It's like new television programs—the networks are so quick to cancel shows that don't immediately attract huge ratings. Some of the most success-ful television programs in history needed a season or two to find their audience. Meaningful partnerships require patience and enough grit to endure the inevitable bumps in the road. Retired Notre Dame football coach Lou Holtz said, "If you don't make a total commitment to what-ever you're doing, then you start looking to bail out the first time the boat starts leaking. It's tough enough getting that boat to shore with everybody rowing, let alone when a guy stands up and starts putting his life jacket on." Stick with the choices you've made, trust that you've se-lected wisely, and commit yourself to making it work.

Commitment requires discipline, and that is something that is hopefully learned very early in life. From the time they were in kinder-garten, my sons understood what was expected of them as students. The watchwords in our home were always (and are still) "First do what you have to do, then do what you want to do." When they came home from school they knew that homework—even simple kindergarten, cut-photographs-out-of-magazines homework—got done before anything else . . . well, almost anything else. They could use the bathroom, wash their hands, and have a glass of water (in that order)—that was it, until they completed their assignments. There was no ambiguity about this. They knew not to ask to watch television, play video games, have a snack, or otherwise goof around until the homework was done. They were both well served by being early adopters of the lessons of self-discipline. The benefits are immeasurable and provide structure and focus in one's professional and personal life in perpetuity.

Children can also learn the value of commitment at a very young age, if they are encouraged by their parents' commitment to their pursuits. Both of my boys were low brass horn players. They began learning on school trombones and French horns, but when it became clear that they were committed to their instruments, it was important to buy them the best professional-quality horns. These serious investments (good horns are very expensive!) reinforced their commitment to their music. They both went on to play All-City, All-State, and in many of Princeton's orchestral groups. When you're all in, it inspires the commitment of others.

Trust yourself and your own judgment enough to commit to whoever and whatever is right for you—regardless of popular opinion. You may not know whom you want to marry or how many children you want to have, but if you ultimately see yourself as a wife and mother (among other things), you need to pursue these goals like a pit bull on a pot roast—or like Lucille in pursuit of a biscuit.

Smart Advice

- Don't be so quick to declare defeat. Sometimes it's smart to double down.
- When you're all in, it inspires the commitment of others.
- The essence of commitment is doing whatever it takes to overcome obstacles.

A Tough Guy from Pleasantville

$\mathcal{B}$E FAITHFUL TO WHO YOU ARE, AND ASPIRE TO HAVE OTHERS SEE you as authentic. You want men who are attracted to you for your true self. I understand that a certain amount of gamesmanship is inherent in courtship, but honestly, keep it to a minimum. How can he know if you are THE ONE or you know if he is THE ONE if neither of you is genuine in your dealings with each other?

Who do you think you're fooling? And why would you attempt to pass yourself off as something other than who you really are? If you are a short Jewish accountant from Long Island, don't try to convince anyone that you are a Clint Eastwood macho man. Nobody will buy it, and you will look delusional. You should be proud of who you are and what you are. If you think your image needs a little tweaking, go ahead . . . tweak away! But be true to yourself and don't compromise your integrity.

Reinventing yourself is certainly a personal prerogative, and some people do so many times in a lifetime. It can be a very good thing— a fresh start if it is organic and consistent with the person you are. In her thirties, Julia Child was a researcher in the Office of Strategic Services during World War II. She learned to cook in her forties and became television's French Chef in her fifties. What our beloved Lady of the Ladle never tried to do was pass herself off as a petite coquette. A croquette maybe . . . but never a coquette.

College is a natural venue for testing a different persona. When I started Princeton, I was eager to be someone other than Susan from the Bronx. So I became "Susie." Freshman week on campus, that's how I introduced myself to everyone I met. I thought it made me sound more effervescent, more interesting, and more fun than Susan. It stuck. Even forty years later, long after I returned to using the more professional name on my birth certificate, when I answer the phone and hear "Susie?" I know it's a college pal, and that makes me smile.

I don't know why at eighteen years old I thought I was insufficiently effervescent, interesting, and fun. Perhaps it was because I didn't take my own mother's advice and diligently practice the piano. I was always a visual artist, never much of a musician. But my mother insisted that I study the piano instead of taking art classes, because, she said, it would make me popular at parties. I wasn't any good at it, but I was a little better than my brother, who also was forced to take the unwanted lessons. Do what you do well. If it matters to you, and you think you might have a natural aptitude, learn a new skill. Despite not knowing how to play the piano, I've always been very popular at parties.

If you are going to try out a new public persona, be honest with yourself about who you really are and how the world will see you. You can tweak your image a little, but the *old* and *new* you shouldn't really be very different. Alvy Singer, the nebbishy protagonist in Woody Allen's classic *Annie Hall*, describes himself as "the balding, virile type." This delusional perspective is as extremely funny as it is obviously ridiculous. The reason that Woody Allen's characters get women as beautiful as Meryl Streep and Diane Keaton is that he's the producer/director of the movie and he casts them (duh). In real life, he's also attracted to gorgeous women because he is a brilliant filmmaker and that makes it easier for attractive girls to see past his scrawny frame and less than classically handsome features. So, unless you have an Academy Award for writing and directing, or are some other kind of luminary, you should probably be more realistic about your expectations and self-image.

Men certainly have no monopoly on *delusional*. Think about women who when seen from behind could be mistaken for teenagers. They sport very long blond hair, micromini skirts, and stiletto heels. But when they slowly turn around, their faces reveal that they are actually closer to one hundred years old than to teenaged. The shock is quite reminiscent of when we finally see Norman Bates's mother in the fruit cellar at the end of *Psycho*. You can't sustain a relationship backward. Eventually, your face will reveal your age as surely as his ridiculous comb-over will one day be windswept. Society places so much focus on youth; it's no wonder that we see so much mutton disguised as lamb. This is a most pitiful kind of false advertising—it's Blanche DuBois counting on the magic of her false youth, instead of living in the reality of her actual age. Embrace your age, whatever it is. It's who you are and is as out of your control as male-pattern baldness. Ponce de Leon never did find the Fountain of Youth, and you are as ready for your close-up as you will ever be, Norma Desmond.

As off-putting as trying to look like someone you're not is claiming to be a maven of things that you know little of. Know what you know, and don't claim authority on subjects and in areas about which you know nothing. Personally, I'm fairly well-read and can converse comfortably on many topics, but there are distinct gaps in my knowledge base. As a deeply rooted New Yorker, I know very little about geography outside Manhattan. Yes, I am aware that there are many states between New York and California, but I couldn't tell you specifically where they are. I am never certain of whether South Montana is north of West Montana, or vice versa. And I know even less about global geography than I do about U.S. geography.

Likewise, I understand nothing about hydroelectric dams or the British monarchy. I have many friends who are dedicated Anglophiles and can sketch the Royal Family tree back to when it was a sapling, but after watching *The Other Boleyn Girl*, I remember thinking that the *surprise* ending was absolutely stunning. Who could have guessed that Anne Boleyn's little red-haired daughter, whose gender was such a disappointment to King Henry VIII, would grow up to be Elizabeth I! Such great writing! This is why I stick to talking about finding a husband, getting married, and having babies.

Talk about what you know. But remember that nobody loves a know-it-all, especially one who knows almost nothing.

Smart Advice

- Be proud of who you are and what you are.
- Go ahead . . . reinvent yourself. But do it authentically.
- Be realistic about your expectations and self-image.

Defining "Having It All"

$\mathcal{I}$T SEEMS THAT TOO MUCH HAS BEEN WRITTEN ABOUT WOMEN HAVing it all. The definition is always heavily skewed toward professional accomplishment, with home and family begrudgingly occupying whatever sliver can be shoved into the equation. If your heartfelt desire is to be a titan of industry, then go for it. Marriage and family aren't for everyone. If it's not for you, then *know* that and dedicate yourself to achieving the components that define *your* personal plan for happiness.

If, however, you know that you want to give birth to your own children, fathered by the man to whom you are married, you absolutely must remain laser focused on your goals and not let anyone or any group attempt to talk you away from what you want. These are basic and natural desires of most women. Neither retrogressive, old-fashioned, nor a betrayal of feminist doctrine, it is *your* life and these are the choices *you* get to make.

Every woman will define "it all" differently. You have to define it for yourself. And that definition will change over time. I had it all twenty years ago, when my babies were little, my home was comfortable, there was money in the bank, and I started a home-based human resources business. Ten years ago, my boys were doing very well in school, my business was doing extraordinarily well (regularly earning more than $350,000 a year from the couch in my living room!), and the flexibility of working from home allowed me to be 100 percent available for my children. I could take them to school, pick them up from school, be class mom, and go on every class trip. My work was invisible to my children. When my younger son was in first grade, I overheard him speaking with his classmates about what everyone's mom did. One said that his mother worked in a bank. One said that his mother worked in a hospital. Another said that her mother was a teacher. When my son was asked what I did, he said, "My mom doesn't do anything. She sits on the couch and talks on the phone."

I have it all again, but the things I have today are different than what I had twenty years ago or ten years ago. I dearly miss having children at home and the peaceful delight of knowing that they were safe and asleep in their beds down the hall. But I now have two grown men whom I watched evolve from infancy into the most amazing adults. I have an extraordinary daughter-in-law and I dream about someday having grandchildren with the same delightful anticipation I had twenty-five years ago when motherhood was on my horizon.

After twenty-seven years, my marriage ended, but now I have the freedom that comes with being a divorced empty-nester. I have a wonderful home that I've reworked, reconfigured, and redecorated over the past twenty-five years to the point that it is now . . . perfect! I *truly* loved the job of parenting more than anything, but without the 24/7 responsibility for taking care of young children, it's amazing how much time there is in the day to do everything and anything else! I can make whatever I want for dinner—or make no dinner—or eat ice cream or a bowl of cereal for dinner. I can watch anything I want on television without anyone making a face. "Ugh, do we *have* to watch *The Good Wife?*" I can put pink towels in my bathroom and fuchsia sheets with flowers and butterflies on my bed. I can go to sleep whenever I want and I have the freedom to invite whomever I choose to my home without any thought to whether my guests are liked by anyone other than me. And I can date wonderful men, with a confidence and comfort that most women in their twenties don't have. I certainly didn't. Honestly, I don't remember ever enjoying dating as much as I do now.

I also have a renewed connection to the university that I love but which I avoided during my marriage to a man who had no interest in Old Nassau. For decades, I missed Princeton and frequently thought that it would have been wonderful to share this special place. When my sons were admitted to Princeton, I felt so blessed, for all the usual reasons that parents are delighted when their children are admitted to their first-choice schools, but especially because it allowed me to embrace the university again and reconnect with it through my sons. Princeton is a constant source of intellectual renewal and social interaction and a reminder of the days when I took my first steps into adulthood.

And now I have a dog named Lucille. She is my first dog, a beautiful dachshund with long red hair, and she goes almost everywhere with me. I used to show people pictures of my boys; now I show them pictures of my dog.

I work with brilliant, beautiful, accomplished women who are executive vice presidents or senior vice presidents of major media companies. They earn in excess of $400,000 per year. They have unlimited travel and entertainment budgets and may even have a wardrobe and salon allowance because their positions require them to look fabulous. As I wear my executive coach hat, these women whom I've known for years come to me for guidance. I ask them if they still feel engaged with the property they work on. They do. I ask if they are still respected and supported by their management. They are. I ask if they feel adequately compensated for their contribution to the business. They certainly do. So, in what way are they dissatisfied? All they have is their work. They are longing for a husband and family. Sadly, most of them are past the age when they are likely to find either.

Remember, you are not a victim of your life . . . you are the architect of your life. Only you know what it means for *you* to have it all. Listen to your inner self.

Define and design the life you want for yourself.

Smart Advice

- Every woman will define "it all" differently.
- You have to define "it all" for yourself.
- How you define "it all" will change over time.

You Say Potatoes . . .

*W*HEN ONE IS CONSIDERING A POTENTIAL LIFE PARTNER, DOES A person's political affiliation really matter? If the marriage of prominent Democrat James Carville and his wife, the very Republican political consultant Mary Matalin, is any indication, maybe it's a good idea to marry someone with opposing political views! Being with someone who holds radically different opinions than your own can be exhilarating—if they aren't just looking for a fight, and they come by their opinions honestly and intelligently.

How does a nice Jewish girl from the Bronx become a Republican? My dad was a lifelong Democrat, as are most middle-class Jews in New York. From the time that he became a United States citizen in 1954, he recognized citizenship to be a special privilege and he voted in every election. Pop was a one-issue voter, and the candidate who was most supportive of Israel got Pop's vote—and that was usually the Democrat. I never thought much about politics as a very young woman, but my desire to go to college—and especially to go *away* to college—labeled me forever and always as a radical progressive in the eyes of my parents.

Of course, in the era of political correctness, anyone who suggests that educated young women think seriously about marriage and motherhood is branded as old-fashioned and retrogressive. My family saw me as ultra-liberal. My more politically correct friends think that I am hopelessly conservative. I don't think of myself as either—I'm a pragmatist and an optimist. Don't let anybody label you; chances are you are a unique combination of many beliefs and opinions, all of which you are entitled to. Few people fall squarely into one camp or another, and there's little need to declare for one party or another until you register to vote. Even then, with the exception of primaries, you vote for the candidate of your choice, regardless of your party. And of course, the completely commitment phobic can register as independent, because they can go only as far as to decide that they can't decide.

So again, how did I become a Republican? Officially, it was junior year, when I was making custom lorgnettes for the fancy ladies of Princeton to match the dresses they were planning to wear to the social event of the 1975 season . . . the McCarter Theatre Masked Ball. Paying my own way through Princeton necessitated the development of many creative ways to earn money. I served lunch to my professors at Prospect (the faculty dining facility), I worked front of house in various theaters on campus, and when the ball was being planned, my artsy nature took over and I constructed an elaborate mask for the chairwoman of the benefit ball committee. She was the mother of a friend in the Class of 1975, and because they lived in town, students frequently visited their home and I got to know her well. She was especially kind to me, and even lent me the dress that I wore to the ball. She loved the mask that I made for her and said that many of her friends would also love masks to match their gowns, and thus a business was born. For a few weeks, my dorm room was converted into a feather-filled factory, with hot-glue guns, faux pearls, and frilly bits of lace and fabric. I produced around 150 masks and earned enough to pay for my junior year tuition. One of my customers was some sort of regional director for the Republican Party in New Jersey, responsible for registering voters. When she came to my dorm room to pick up her mask and pay me, she asked if I was a registered voter. At the time, I was not. She had the registration forms with her. I signed up, she paid me, everybody was happy. The ball was a smashing success and I recognized everyone there—behind the masks that I made especially for them.

I had thought about my political affiliation long before that. Sometime during my senior year in high school, I was with my mentor (a Princetonian from the Class of 1959 who was my alumni interviewer) and his wife, who told me casually that she was a Republican because she believed that if you work hard, are successful, and earn a lot of money, you should be able to enjoy the fruits of your labors and not have to give so much of it to the government in taxes. With what part of that can you argue? It sounded right to me. It still does, and not because I am averse to paying taxes. Again, I think about my pop, who would frequently say that he wished he had to pay a million dollars to the government every April 15—because if that was his tax liability, how successful must he be!

Beware of people who say things like "I would *never* watch Fox News." What they are basically telling you is that they would never consider an opinion other than their own. These sanctimonious bloviators are usually ill-informed and small-minded. Never say never! There may well be topics and issues that are better covered by a more conservative perspective . . . or not. If you wouldn't even consider that coverage, then you'll never know! Similarly, advice like Ann Coulter's *How to Talk to a Liberal (If You Must)* is obviously dismissive of opinions, without the benefit of actually hearing them—but at least Ann Coulter is usually an amusing read.

Political lines don't seem to be drawn with the clarity that existed in previous generations. The designation of Democrat versus Republican is murky: RINOs, DINOs, Reagan Democrats, Obama Republicans. Resist the temptation to pigeonhole others and be cautious around people who would hurl labels at you rather than listen to what you have to say. You know who among your friends leans toward conservatism and who is more liberal. You probably will agree on some issues but not all. It is this healthy exchange of ideas that provides the greatest opportunities for learning and growth. Learn from all of them.

A conservative Jewish Republican from the Bronx, or a liberal Christian Democrat from the South . . . it doesn't really matter if you say potatoes and I say pot*ah*toes, as long as we can sit down to dinner together.

Smart Advice

- One man's (liberal) trash is another man's (conservative) treasure.
- Don't let others define you. Define yourself.
- Keep an open mind. Never say never.

Before You Cut the End
off the Roast Beef

*T*HINK ABOUT WHAT YOU'RE DOING BEFORE YOU DO IT. MAKE SURE that it makes sense to you. If it doesn't make sense, don't do it! You're a smart girl. It's not like you don't recognize the words. For instance, you want to be married and have children, but the media is bombarding you with messages about how educated women should focus only on professional achievement and working harder. Does that make sense to you? It certainly doesn't make sense *for* you. The zeitgeist, or prevailing attitude toward women's mandate to climb the corporate ladder, can be oppressive for women who aspire to the traditional roles of wife and mother. But you know what you want for yourself, and an alarm should go off in your head every time marriage and motherhood are disparaged.

Don't be so quick to accept everything you hear or follow every instruction you are given. Think for yourself. If something doesn't sound right to you—question it. Respectfully, and within reason, ask for clarification until it makes sense to you. Understand that sometimes the people instructing you may not understand themselves why they are directing you as they are. They may be blindly following instructions given to them. When you ask the question "Why are we doing it this way?" and the answer is "Because that's the way it's always been done," then you know that you are dealing with a nonthinker. Be smarter for yourself about what you do and the choices you make.

As you focus on your goals, be sure that you understand why you do what you do to achieve them. Don't be complacent. If it doesn't feel right, it probably isn't. Think about what doesn't feel authentic to you and course-correct accordingly.

Of course, there are times that we all do seemingly illogical things out of force of habit, or because it is comforting to those around us to follow certain protocols. I can't explain why, but the use of any amount of Scotch tape makes me anxious. I suppose there must have been an episode in my childhood where I got into trouble for using too much of it. I don't remember, but watching anyone dispense long strips of tape makes me grit my teeth. This is just a silly individual quirk that doesn't mean much, or have any serious consequences. What you need to be conscious of are the nonsensical choices you make (and sometimes repeatedly make) that could change the arc of your life in ways that you may not realize soon enough to make a meaningful course correction.

Do your romantic relationships usually end with your asking your best friend, "Why do I always gravitate to men who treat me horribly?"

Well . . . why do you? What are you thinking? Or, are you *not* thinking at all?

We all occasionally make a bad choice, but if you have a history of one bad relationship after another, I urge you to seriously examine what is drawing you in these unfruitful directions. Perhaps you need to talk with someone—your parents, clergy, a trusted friend, or other professional who may be able to shed light on where you are going wrong. If you are regularly dating people, or keep friends who are bad *for* you or *to* you, then you are either not paying attention to what you're doing or just don't understand what you're doing. It's important that you afford yourself a deep think about this, because if you want to know what you are committed to having in this life—just look at what you've got. If you are very clear about what you want and what you don't want, then you're more likely to focus your efforts productively and know what justifies your walking away.

Sometimes we do odd things because we are respecting long-established customs, and I'm all for honoring traditions. But think about why you do what you do and why you make the choices that you make. That your family has a history of dysfunction is no excuse for your relationship failures. There is no such thing as a family tradition of poor relationship choices. You're smarter than that. Make better choices for yourself and understand the choices you make.

There is a story about a young bride, eager to prepare a nice dinner for her new husband and calling her mother to ask how to make roast beef. The mother tells her daughter, "Cut the end off the meat, season it well with salt and pepper, and roast it in the oven at three hundred seventy-five degrees for an hour." The daughter asks why she should cut the end off the meat. The mother says, "I don't really know, but that's the way Grandma always made it." Realizing that she too didn't really understand the logic in this, the mother called her *own* mother to ask. "Ma, why did you cut the end off the roast beef before you put it in the oven?" Grandma replied, "Well, we used to have a very small oven."

The prevailing wisdom of a time gone by may have no place in the life that you lead today. What was once logical and practical may no longer make sense. Think about what you are doing and understand why you are doing it.

It's sometimes hard to know whom to turn to for counsel. Most of the time, parents are a good resource. Even if you don't always agree with them, they want what's good for you. Don't allow yourself to be influenced by people who may not have your best interests at heart, or by those who are well-intentioned but ignorant. They may try to be helpful but don't know what they are talking about or what you really need. In the final analysis, you are responsible for your own happiness. When you consider your choices, make sure that they make sense to you— before you cut the end off the roast beef.

Gracie Allen's Advice for How to Cook Roast Beef

1. Get two roast beefs, one big one and one little one.
2. Put them both in a hot oven.
3. When the little one is burnt, the big one is done.

Say good night, Gracie.

Smart Advice

- If something doesn't sound right to you—question it.
- Don't be complacent. If it doesn't feel right, it probably isn't.
- If you understand what you think, and why you do what you're doing, you're better able to find what you want.

To Forgive . . . It's Divine

*H*E FORGOT YOUR BIRTHDAY, BROKE YOUR FAVORITE MUG, CANCELED his date with you to hang out with his friends, used your toothbrush without asking, and stepped on your dog. Okay, how willing are you to forgive him these trespasses? If you can do so with a good heart, then he may very well be THE ONE.

Forgiveness is an attribute of the strong, and our ability and willingness to forgive is a very reliable indicator of our true feelings about others. When we are in love we can forgive the worst transgressions. But if we've lost our love for someone, we can't overlook even the most insignificant offenses. When the party is *really* over, the little quirks and peculiarities we once found charming will grate on us. If you come to a point where you can't forgive him for snoring, being short, or being bald . . . your relationship is done. There is a reason why forgiveness factors so heavily in religious doctrine. In many ways, it defines who we are and what we genuinely love.

We're supposed to forgive. The Bible says so: Bear with each other and forgive whatever grievances you may have against one another.

It's an act of faith in humanity. We forgive in the hopes that when we err, we too will be forgiven. Even the most conscientious among us will occasionally misstep. The only people who don't make mistakes are people who don't do anything. Owning up to your mistakes requires courage. When you have erred, be the first to say so and put forward the facts as you know them—it's called spin control. Most errors are eventually discovered, so don't wait for the sword of Damocles to fall on your head while hoping that nobody noticed what you did wrong. Living one step ahead of the sheriff's bullet is miserable; it will rob you of sleep and keep you from thinking clearly. Okay, so you blew it. Stand up, take responsibility, make necessary corrections and apologies—and move on!

The holiest day of the Jewish calendar is Yom Kippur, also known as the Day of Atonement, when Jews are commanded to actively seek forgiveness from those we have wronged. Our hearts are lightened and our heads are cleared when we circle back to acknowledge that we have done wrong and are pardoned by those we may have harmed. And of course, forgiveness also factors heavily in Christian teaching. Dying on the cross, Jesus asks for forgiveness for those who crucified him. From the gospel of Luke: *Father, forgive them; for they know not what they do.*

Here's the problem . . . people who are *constantly* apologizing. Are their apologies really intended to assuage their *own* guilt, or are they truly expressing regret for any pain, inconvenience, or hurt feelings they caused others? It's probably the first. While most of us appreciate the retrospection that precipitates an apology, wouldn't we much prefer that the offenders be more thoughtful to begin with? Recidivist offenders seem to not really care about what they're doing or how their actions affect others. They do what they want, and if there is any blowback, they apologize. It's as if they regard an apology as a license to steal. Think before you act. Be considerate. No apologies necessary!

Almost as vexing are the people who are *endlessly* apologizing. They beg your pardon for walking in front of the TV screen, for taking the last roll on the dinner table, for brushing your arm ever so lightly in reaching for the remote control. Life is too short to be apologizing for the air you breathe.

Any discussion of apologies and of forgiveness requires acknowledgment of these basic truths. Just as an apology does more for the *offender* than the *offended*—forgiveness serves the *forgiver* more than the *forgiven*. And as Oscar Wilde said, "Always forgive your enemies; nothing annoys them so much."

To truly forgive requires that you also forget. It's not unlike a loan that is forgiven—it no longer requires being paid back. It's as if the loan was never made. If you don't forget an insult or transgression, then you're not really forgiving. You might be putting it aside, but it remains in your memory. Self-preservation and learning from our past vulnerabilities demand that we not ever forgive completely. As a child of two Holocaust survivors, I remember *Lest we forget* being so frequently intoned at home, it might as well have been embroidered on a pillow in the living room.

Perhaps most difficult is forgiving yourself, the wisdom of Ralph Kramden notwithstanding. In an early episode of *The Honeymooners*, Ralph and his best friend, Ed Norton, are at odds when Ed is dispatched on some dangerous mission in the bowels of the sewer system where he is employed. Wife Alice encourages Ralph to put the petty argument aside and assist his friend, saying, "If anything happened to Ed, you would hate yourself." Ralph replies, "Not for long. I have a very forgiving nature."

If you are going to forgive others, do so sincerely and with grace. I learned from my father how alleviating another's guilt before they can even muster the courage to ask for forgiveness can make you a hero. When my parents came to America in 1949 they had been married for almost four years and began their new life in a walk-up apartment on the

Lower East Side of Manhattan. Pop, eager to assimilate and always one to root for the underdog, soon became an avid Brooklyn Dodgers fan and was crestfallen when they moved to California. Ma worked hard at being a good homemaker and caring for my older brother. At the time, she had a very modest diamond ring that Pop had bought for her in Germany with the meager wages he had earned from working with the American troops that liberated the camps and helped resettle the survivors. Once, when Ma was doing the dishes, she took off her ring, wrapped it in a paper napkin, and put it on the windowsill above the sink for safekeeping. Her older sister, my aunt Sally, was living with my parents at the time. She obviously didn't know that Ma's ring was in the napkin, and trying to help clean the kitchen, my aunt threw it out. Ma was heartbroken and dreaded having to tell Pop what had happened. She eventually did, and Pop's response was "I'm more upset that the Dodgers have left Brooklyn."

He couldn't forgive Walter O'Malley for moving his beloved Dodgers to the west coast, but he forgave my mother. This happened long before I was born, but I will forever remember my mother telling me this story, and my Pop for this amazingly generous expression of love and forgiveness.

Smart Advice

- An apology is not a license to steal.
- Successful relationships frequently require forgiveness.
- If you can't forgive him for things he has no control over, stick a fork in it . . . your relationship is done.

I Knew You Were Coming, so I Baked a Cake

$\mathcal{A}$CTUALLY, I PROBABLY BAKED A PIE. DESPITE A VERY WELL-appointed kitchen, I don't have good cake pans, but I do have pie plates of every size. There is also just something special and homey about a pie. It conjures up images of an apron-clad mom placing a lattice-crusted, fruit-filled beauty on a windowsill to cool. Without entering into the fray of the great "pie versus cake debate," let it suffice to say that I usually serve homemade pie for dessert when I have dinner parties.

Husbands used to score professional points by bringing the boss home for a home-cooked meal. That doesn't seem to happen very much anymore, but families still take great pride in their gracious wife/mom who creates a home that is warm, welcoming, nourishing, and fun. I know . . . it sounds a bit like June Cleaver, but who didn't love Beaver's mom?

If you aspire to traditional homemaking, you had better learn how to cook!

Is the way to a man's heart through his stomach? It's certainly one of the ways.

It seems to have become a lost art, but entertaining at home is one of life's great joys. Sharing your home, your food, and your labors with friends is incredibly soul satisfying. Don't know how to cook? No excuse—if you can read, you can cook. Foolproof recipes are available on hundreds of websites, in magazines and newspapers, and your mother probably has a terrific meat loaf recipe she'd share with you. Successful entertaining is much more about being a great host than being a great cook.

When planning your menu, it doesn't have to be fancy cuisine, but it has to be plentiful, well prepared, and served with a genuine warmth that makes your guests feel nourished by both the food and your hospitality. Here's the tacit agreement . . . they will give up their time and give you the home court advantage, and you will welcome them warmly and not send them home hungry. It's that simple.

Perhaps because everyone spends so much time at the office, the thought of extending invitations, planning menus, shopping, cooking, and serving a meal seems overwhelming. Once you've done it a few times, you'll see that it really isn't. Honestly, preparing a meal doesn't take nearly as long as cleaning the house—and you know that you have to clean the house anyway. That bathroom isn't going to clean itself!

Dining with friends at home is a very different and in many ways better experience than having a meal in a restaurant. To start with, the cost of preparing a meal is a fraction of menu prices. When did a *glass* of wine become fourteen dollars at a restaurant? And, instead of being told by the reservation warden when you can eat dinner ("We can seat you at nine forty-five"), and being interrupted by waiters with pepper grinders, you can control the evening leisurely and for as long as everyone is having a good time. No one is waiting for your table.

Everything I know about being a gracious hostess I learned from my best friend's mother. When we were students at Princeton and spent vacation weeks in her Westport home, Mrs. Crolius would welcome me as lovingly and enthusiastically as if I were her own daughter. Forty years later, she still does.

If you are truly happy to share your home with your guests, they will feel it. You don't need to be a great cook or have a perfectly appointed home—just enough food, drink, dinnerware, flatware, glassware, and chairs. And nothing has to match, as long as it's clean and functional. It's okay . . . it's your home, not a restaurant. I remember once planning a dinner party and being flummoxed by wanting to invite a few more guests than I had forks for. My brilliant young son resolved my conundrum by wisely suggesting, "Ma, buy more forks." I did. They didn't match my other forks, and it couldn't have mattered less.

In addition to having wonderful times, great conversations, and creating fond memories, successful entertaining at home builds personal confidence. It hones your organizational skills, reinforces friendships, and establishes *your* home as the place where people love to congregate.

The more you entertain at home, the better you'll get at it. In fact, you can get *too* confident. Many years ago, I was having a New Year's Eve dinner party and had become so adept at completing every detail of the evening in advance that by five o'clock I was all done! Guests were due to arrive at eight, so with three unscheduled hours before company arrived, I opened a bottle of champagne. Never one to tolerate alcohol well, by five thirty my head was spinning very badly and all I wanted to do was sleep. I was so intoxicated that I couldn't imagine being sober enough to welcome guests in a couple of hours (or ever). Thankfully, a brief nap, some strong coffee, and a cool shower brought me back to life that night. Happy New Year!

I especially love multigenerational dinner parties, gatherings of my friends and classmates with their children, who are often friends and classmates of my children. It ensures a plurality of opinions and the kids can usually be conscripted to clear the table and load the dishwasher. In fairness, when my son hosts his friends in our home, I am frequently nothing more than the kitchen wench and scullery maid.

Bringing people together in your home for a lovingly prepared meal and to enjoy each other's company is both a joy and a *mitzvah* (a good deed). To break bread with friends is a sacred experience that connects you to others.

Host a dinner party—make memories, take photos, and bake a cake . . . or a pie.

Great Meat Loaf Recipe
(in case your mother won't give you hers)

3 lbs. ground beef	2 tablespoons mustard
1 cup dried bread crumbs	2 tablespoons salt
1 chopped onion	½ teaspoon pepper
¼ cup brown sugar	Handful of minced parsley
¼ cup ketchup	

1. Combine ingredients and form into a loaf.
2. Bake at 350°F degrees for an hour.

Smart Advice

- You want to be a great wife and mother? Learn to cook!

- Home cooking nourishes the body and soul like nothing else.

- Yes, the way to a man's heart is through his stomach.

PART V

Wise Advice for Wise Women

Smart girls become wise women—sooner or later.

Arguably, the greater virtue is common sense, or street smarts. Whether you're married, single, still single, or single again, you learn, if you are smart, that there is more to life than family, more to life than just work. There is life: your life, *the life you lead. It is about knowing yourself and respecting yourself and owning who you are at any age.*

Maturity—It's Better than the Alternative

*S*OMETIMES YOU JUST HAVE NO IDEA WHAT AWAITS YOU UNTIL YOU get where you're going. I would have laughed if anyone had told me that dating in your fifties is absolutely wonderful! But it truly is. If you are celebrating twenty-five years or more of married bliss . . . good for you! But if you are single again as a result of divorce or widowhood, or have always been single, you may be delighted by the extraordinary discovery of grown-up dating. This is the amazing revelation: When you're *not* looking for a man to marry and be the father of your children . . . WOW . . . it is so much fun to just enjoy men for who they are. It's fabulous!

For most young women, dating is very much like interviewing applicants to choose a good tax preparer or housekeeper, except it's for the most important job opening of your life—your husband. Candidates are evaluated based on many criteria: past performance (where have they been?), track record (what have they done?), cultural fitness (are they age-appropriate and do they share your religious affinity?), availability (are they single?), presentation and comportment (do they look good and carry themselves positively and comfortably?), communication skills (can they actively participate in a cogent conversation about meaningful subjects?), etc.

In truth, in your twenties you are evaluating your dates for much *more* than just the position of your husband . . . you are looking for a father for your future children. Finding the best possible man (and genetic material) for your offspring is an enormous responsibility. I remember dating after college and trying to imagine what these men would look like with a baby in their arms, or changing a diaper, or coaching a Little League team. Would he be a good role model if we had sons? Would he be selfless enough to put our children's needs before his own? How would his family's medical history impact the health of our future children? Almost more important than what kind of husband would he be—what kind of father would he be? Actually, it is more important. You may have more than one husband in your lifetime. Your children will have only one biological father.

Without consciously thinking about it, all young women impose these long-term planning and forecasting scenarios on their dates. Because it is so extremely important to choose your future children's father wisely, the carefree joy of dating is somewhat diminished. Thankfully, most young women aren't even aware of that unless and until they start dating again much later in life and realize that their date's fatherhood potential is no longer a consideration.

I couldn't have imagined how liberating it is to date as a grown woman. Many mature men are worldly and accomplished. Many of them are financially secure and well mannered. Some have sense enough to wear something other than blue jeans sometimes, and some even know how attractive they look in a well-tailored suit. They can be secure enough in their life's accomplishments to not be threatened by a formidable woman. In fact, they love being with women who are powerful, self-possessed, and happy. They know what a delight it is to be out with them.

Needless to say, not all mature men are that wonderful. In some cases, calling them "mature" is misleading. They are just old boys who never outgrew their selfishness, childishness, and immaturity. I always marvel at older men who crave the company of *much* younger women. I understand that the geezer thinks the twenty-six-year-old trophy wife on his arm makes him look like a virile stud, but doesn't it really make him look like a foolish old guy with a gold-digger? The good news is that these grown-up narcissists, along with the grown-up whiners and the grown-up male drama queens, are a minority. Most men in their fifties or older have lived long enough to know better. And they *love* women who are happy to be with them.

It's probably fair to say that older daters have probably been divorced. In many cases, they're divorced after decades of marriage to the same person. Perhaps part of the joy of mature dating is just being with someone (anyone!) other than the person from whom you were divorced and had grown tired of over the decades. Without the baggage that accompanied your marriage, dating is a clean slate. It's an opportunity to start again, have fun again, and maybe fall in love again!

If you haven't dated in a long while, you've probably forgotten how much fun it is to flirt, and be flirted with. If done with finesse, it can make you feel like a teenager, and it can remind you of how attractive you still are . . . even at your age and even after all of these years.

Speaking of attractiveness . . . if you are going to embark upon a new dating chapter in your adult life, do everything you can to prepare yourself for a successful experience. Girls, lose the weight! I know it's hard . . . just do it.

Fix and whiten your teeth.

See a good hairdresser and find an updated hairstyle that suits you.

Buy a new outfit or two that you would look forward to wearing on a date.

Maybe you could use a new fragrance? I had a drawer full of perfume bottles that were in varying states of empty. They were all decades old. I don't know whether perfume actually deteriorates over time, but all of the bottles in my drawer collectively and individually started to smell like "old lady." Treat yourself to a new fragrance.

Do what you can to feel good about yourself and how you look. Self-confidence on a date is very attractive. And be of good cheer. Do not complain about your ex, your children, your medical condition, or anything else. Being happy on a date is a powerful aphrodisiac.

Of course, if you are dating in your fifties or older, you should still be cognizant of many of the same criteria as very young women. Look for good men, kind men, ones who can express logical and intelligent thoughts.

But when you are *past* your childbearing years and not evaluating father material, dating is a whole different experience than it was decades earlier. It's fun. You are no longer distracted by the sound of a ticking biological clock. You are no longer afraid of an unwanted pregnancy.

And it doesn't even matter if he's not Jewish! Or even if he is!

Smart Advice

- You're done having babies. The men you date are just for you!
- Powerful, self-possessed, and happy women are a huge turn-on for grown men.
- Start dating again, have fun again, fall in love again! Go on. You've earned it!

Count on It—Plan for It

$\mathscr{H}$OW IS IT THAT GROWN WOMEN REACH THEIR FIFTIES AND EXPRESS shock and regret that their baby birds have left the nest, and now they don't know what to do with their lives?

Really? Did you honestly not see that coming?

Surely you didn't think that your babies would be babies forever. When you gave birth, wasn't it with the understanding that you would love, nurture, and raise your infants to someday become capable, responsible adults who would go out on their own and care for themselves? Unless you've discovered some miraculous secret to stabilize or reverse the aging process, you should have known that you would someday be in your fifties, and that it would come thirty years after your twenties, twenty years after your thirties, and ten years after your forties. This doesn't require an advanced degree in mathematics, girls. You had to know that this day was coming. Once your kids are grown and your primary responsibilities for raising children are behind you, your days will be spent very differently than they were when you were checking homework and packing school lunches.

Women who bemoan feeling useless now that their children are grown and they are middle-aged are a lot like people who are caught unaware and unprepared on April 15, when taxes are due at the Internal Revenue Service. It's pretty predictable. It comes at the same time every year.

Could you truly not have anticipated this?

If you were fortunate enough to have had the luxury to stay home with your young children, I sincerely hope you did so. And if you did, I hope you loved it as much as I did, and that you have an indelible bank of wonderful memories that comfort and delight you on those days when you're missing your babies. And I sincerely hope that while you were home with your children, you gave some thought to how you would positively and productively use your newfound free time when your children were grown.

You might be thinking about reentering the workforce. Let me take off my Princeton Mom kerchief, put on my Human Resources Professional hat, and tell you the truth about getting hired in your fifties when you haven't worked in decades.

It almost never happens.

Some industries are more welcoming of a *mature* workforce than others, but most businesses are image-conscious and are interested in putting a youthful face on their staff. Financial management and the legal profession are more tolerant of an older workforce because of the gravitas factor—clients of these businesses are comforted to think that older and wiser people are overseeing their financial and legal needs. But industries like advertising, marketing, and media are all about image, and the presidents of the biggest players in these businesses are all under fifty. If they would even consider hiring your fifty-five-year-old self (and I seriously doubt that they would), it would only be for a position that would probably be so junior that your ego couldn't tolerate it.

We can all continue to hope for an improved economy, but while it remains sluggish, the reality is that there are very few open positions and there is very little hiring going on. And people who are younger and considerably more affordable than you will very likely fill those limited positions that do open up.

Please don't even *think* about blaming your diminished hireability on your children, or the fact that you removed yourself from the workforce to raise them. The truth is that if you didn't stay home with your children, and remained on the job, by the time you reached your fifties you'd likely be downsized. Again, there are younger, less expensive employees who could probably do your job, and everyone loves bright young faces in the office. Either way, you'd now be unemployed and virtually unemployable. But at least you would have had the precious gift of being with your children when they needed you most.

Planning for your post-parenting, pre-retirement years requires dedicated and creative thought. If you're smart and clever this can be an incredibly exciting time and an opportunity to dramatically expand your network of friends. And depending on your skills and ambition, you could earn some very serious money. When my first son was days away from being born, I left my job as the director of executive recruitment for Arthur Andersen in New York. When my second son was about to enter kindergarten and I knew that soon, and for the first time in almost eight years, I would have unscheduled time, I thought about what I could do. To productively fill the hours when both of my children were in school, I started doing industrial research for magazine publishers. I scoured mastheads and called in to companies to gather and confirm information about their organizational structure and personnel. Human resources departments used this information for recruiting purposes, and paid me well for it . . . $160 per hour. I then took on the recruitment function, a job very well suited to being performed from home.

Later, I served many human resources departments in a broader consulting capacity. Becoming an executive coach was an obvious and natural extension of the candidate consultation that I'd done for years as an executive recruiter.

If you've already been married and successfully raised your children, now I'm *all* in favor of your focusing on your career. Start a business, write your memoir, go back to school. Think creatively and commit yourself to a new chapter in profitable productivity. If money isn't an issue . . . lucky you! Learn to knit, take up gardening, do volunteer work, make your own goat cheese!

Assuming you do a good job bringing up your children to be independent adults, and you don't meet with an untimely demise, you *will* someday be an empty-nester in your fifties.

You can count on it. You had better plan for it.

How to Make Homemade Goat Cheese

1. Milk a goat until you have about a quart (or, for the less industrious, buy a quart).
2. Simmer the milk with some lemon juice and salt to taste.
3. Pour it into a cheesecloth bag and hang it up.
4. Let the excess drip for about an hour.

Enjoy!

Smart Advice

- You now have discretionary time. Use it wisely and productively.

- Maybe you're an entrepreneur?

- Learn a new skill, run for office, or write a book!

Parents, Talk with Your Daughters!

*W*HAT ARE YOU WAITING FOR? WHAT ARE YOU AFRAID OF? I KNOW, you haven't spoken with your daughter about finding a husband and starting a family because you think that at best, she'll roll her eyes impatiently and dismiss you with an exasperated "Oh, Mom." Or she'll accuse you of being old-fashioned, out of touch with the realities of modern women, and generally meddlesome. While not heartwarming responses, they are not the end of the world. If your daughter dreams of a traditional home and family but misses her best chance to find the love of her life, get married, and have children . . . yes, that *is* cataclysmic. She is being bombarded with feminist rhetoric to avoid marriage and think only about her career, and by her girlfriends who are regularly engaging in hookups and casual sex. Who is going to tell your daughter that she has to be smarter for herself than that? I'm trying to . . . but this is a message that *must* be reinforced by *you*. Daughters need to be reminded of the realities: the limitations of their fertility, the importance of finding a husband while their options are plentiful, and that men are lacking incentive to commit to a relationship when they are regularly offered sex without commitment. If they lose sight of these things and tragically forfeit their dreams, they'll never forgive themselves . . . and neither will you for not reminding them of what is really important to them. Let everyone else maintain politically correct gentility; this is your daughter! Tell her what she needs to hear—and keep telling her.

When I was a college student, I had a few classmates whose parents not only didn't object to their children's excessive drinking and marijuana smoking, but, attempting to be seen as cool, were in fact enablers of their kids' use of these substance. Parents who act as suppliers and underwriters of potentially addictive and illegal behavior are not acting in their children's best interests. Instead of being thought of as cool and progressive, these parents are actually regarded as misguided and a bit pathetic. Your underage children don't need you to be an overage friend buying their booze or reefer—they all know how to score these substances without your assistance. You may not be able to discourage your children's use of them, but you need to remain the responsible adult. Even worse are parents who pull up to the smoker's circle and toke a joint along with their kids. Your participation encourages them unduly; it's better to relive your youth with your own friends than grasp at *relevance* by getting high with your kids.

Okay, so your daughter brings her boyfriend home during winter break. Can he stay with her in her room? No, he cannot. She may not fully understand the psychodynamics of potential buyers walking away from a sale if the merchandise is available for free, but don't you? This isn't complicated game theory. It doesn't require John Nash's beautiful mind to understand how disincentivizing it is for young men to commit to your daughter when she offers him sex without commitment. By accepting it, you're encouraging it.

I was recently talking with the parents of one of my son's classmates on campus. She's a lovely girl whom I've gotten to know, and I was delighted to meet her family. I told them that if their daughter's summer internship in the city ever keeps her beyond a reasonable hour to travel back to their suburban home, she is very welcome to stay with me. They were appreciative, but said that if it came to that, she would probably stay with her boyfriend, who also lives in Manhattan. I asked whether they were okay with that. Their answer was "Not really, but what can we do?" You can say *no*. Discourage your daughter from doing what you know isn't good for her. She may do it anyway, but if not you, who is going to tell her the truth about why she doesn't help herself by giving it away?

Expect your kids to disregard a good amount of what you say about almost everything. It is the nature of children to question the wisdom of their parents, who they know are not infallible. My folks told me some ridiculous things when I was very young. We weren't very observant, but rather than explaining to me the principles of kashrut (Jewish religious laws concerning the suitability of food), they said simply that we didn't eat ham because pork makes you stupid. Regardless of the fact that much of your advice will land on your children's deaf ears, you might get lucky and have some of your knowledge infiltrate their psyches, despite themselves. They are smart enough to know that even a blind pig finds a truffle every once in a while. But is that blind pig kosher? Clearly, I'm the wrong one to ask.

Chances are that there have been many times in your children's lives when you had to intervene to make sure that their long-term interests were protected, even at the expense of their short-term inconvenience, objections, and resentment. At eleven years old, they didn't ask for braces on their teeth, but you knew that they needed them to ensure a healthy bite and an attractive smile in adulthood. So you schlepped them to the orthodontist and insisted that they wear the rubber bands that flung food across the dining room at mealtime, while they pulled that overbite into shape. You know what your children need, even when they don't.

When she enters college, your daughter will never again be as young, as beautiful, as attractive to men, or as fertile. Encourage her to make the best use of this time. Instead of listening to politically correct rhetoric, she should be listening to you. Go on! Risk offending her for an hour on a quiet afternoon. If she hears you, the rewards could change her whole life. You must set boundaries for your kids. Until they are fully launched in their adult lives, they need your guidance, regardless of how much they may protest.

Don't be afraid to be a parent. Your children won't love you any less, and they may respect you even more.

Smart Advice

- Step up to the parenting plate and tell your daughters the truth.
- Tell her what she needs to hear—and keep telling her.
- Discourage your daughter from doing what you know isn't good for her. She needs to hear it from someone!

You Know What?
This Is Who I Am and
This Is What I Was Thinking

$\mathcal{S}$INCE MY LETTER FIRST APPEARED IN THE *DAILY PRINCETONIAN*, I'VE been asked many times about whether I ever imagined that it would create such an international firestorm. No, I certainly did not. It would have been absurd to think that a few words of motherly advice in my school newspaper would hit such a nerve around the world, and create so many opportunities for extended conversations about topics that had been shied away from for decades. When I wrote it, I had hoped it would inspire women undergraduates at Princeton who want to marry and have children, to start planning for their personal happiness with the same dedication and commitment they are investing in planning for their professional success—and to think about maybe finding their husbands on campus. Why not? It's the greatest concentration of single, age-appropriate, well-educated, and similarly motivated men that they will ever be among.

How widespread a commotion did my letter cause? In very quantifiable terms, I am told that it received in excess of 100 million Internet inquiries . . . within two days of its publication. In comparison, the shooting of schoolchildren in Newtown, Connecticut, received a bit more than 10 million inquiries. How could it be that my folksy advice generated ten times more interest than one of the deadliest mass shootings in American history? It's because the tragic death of American students didn't *directly* affect China, Japan, India, Pakistan, England, Australia, Israel, and many other countries around the world. But families in all of these countries and more are very, very concerned about their well-educated daughters marrying smart and having families of their own, before it's too late. Many of these families send their brilliant girls to the United States to be educated and perhaps also find husbands while they are here.

Many of these parents, as well as their daughters and educated young women on Princeton's campus and on other campuses, have written to tell me how eager they have been to discuss marriage and motherhood, but didn't even know how to broach the topics. Obviously, this is a conversation that has been long overdue and seriously needed to be initiated. I never intended to be a lightning rod, but okay . . . if it gets the conversation going.

I've also never been a writer. My college roommates were (and still are) writers, but I've enjoyed the process of putting these words on paper. I've especially enjoyed the television appearances, and am appreciative of the onstage training I got with the Princeton Triangle Club so many years ago. When the media attention began, which was almost instantly, I was wisely counseled by a very media-savvy friend and client to "do it all, just don't let anyone make you say anything that you don't believe." That was very useful advice. The opinions that I have expressed I have held for a very long time; they are absolutely heartfelt, and so thoroughly intended for good that I never feared the *gotcha* question, nor has any of the vitriolic commentary been personally troubling. As my pop used to say, "It's great to be an American . . . you can have your opinion and I can have mine."

Obviously, there is no single *right* way to plan for personal happiness. Everyone is different and each individual circumstance requires examination, consideration, and a methodology for achieving one's life's goals. You have to be smart for yourself and find your own personal path to happiness.

A few days after my letter was published in the *Daily Princetonian*, I wrote this follow-up letter to the women of Princeton:

Now That I Know I Have Your Attention . . .

It seemed to me that all of the wisdom that was being offered to you focused only on your professional development. I take it as a given that you will have a successful career that puts your many talents to productive use. The advice I offer is intended to encourage you to pursue a more holistic approach to fulfilling your life's dreams—if those dreams include bearing children in a traditional marriage. I want to encourage you to take full advantage of everything Princeton has to offer: a world-class education, as well as a community of people who share your appreciation for academic excellence and an intellectual curiosity. You have an extraordinary opportunity to find lifelong friends, and maybe a life partner with whom to form a family and raise children. If that's what you want, I am suggesting that you multi-task during these undergraduate years.

This thinking is neither anti-feminist nor retrogressive. It's practical. Simply put, there is not gender equality in all matters. The window of opportunity for men to marry and have children is almost limitless. You don't have that kind of time.

In the 1950s, women were encouraged to find a husband early

because opportunities for women in the workforce were limited. They had few options, so they married after college and spent the next ten to fifteen years having children. If after graduating, you spend the next ten to fifteen years invested only in professional development, you will find yourself in your thirties and may have nothing but your career, limited marriage prospects, and a loudly ticking biological clock. Interesting how the same advice (find a husband early) is meaningful today, but for different reasons. Pursue all of your dreams—not just the ones that are politically popular. And don't be afraid to want what you want. Don't be shouted down by those who want you to want what they want—instead of all you want for yourselves.

To those of you who have written to me to express your thanks for my confirming what you've been thinking, but were afraid to say out loud, I sincerely appreciate your thoughtfulness. No thanks were necessary, nor were your apologies. I understood why you messaged me privately.

Obviously, the opinions I express are my own, and as with any advice . . . you can take it or not. I wish you continued success and every happiness.

Keep talking!

Susan Patton, Class of 1977

Acknowledgments

I'm not a writer. Well, I suppose that now I am.

The writing of this book was enabled by the assistance and encouragement of many friends and colleagues. I am sincerely appreciative of the wonderful people at Simon & Schuster who helped me navigate this unfamiliar terrain: Jen Bergstrom, Louise Burke, Jennifer Robinson, Liz Psaltis, Al Madocs, Tim Pitoniak, Chelsea McGukin, Ellen Chan, Davina Mock, Kevin McCahill, and especially the ever-patient Natasha Simons.

It was particularly joyous to work with my editor and classmate, Mitchell Ivers. We met more than forty years ago as freshmen at Princeton, and because he's known my voice since we were eighteen, he was able to help me find it authentically for this book.

Many thanks to my agent, Jane Dystel, and her team at Dystel & Goderich Literary Management.

Very special thanks to so many dear friends and classmates for their support and encouragement, including Kendall Crolius, Gwendolyn Fortson Waring, Carol Wallace, Marilyn Martin, Beth Adler, Linda Pirolli, Marian Levy Phillips, Donna Freeman, Susanne Tufts, Ellen

Eifrig Rennard, Lori Cherup, Christine Caffrey, Lisa Gornick, Arline Geronimus, Jill Smolowe, Joanne Muratori, Laurie Rosenwasser, Jill Baron, Fred Doar, Tom Gerson, David Michaelis, Victor Simpkins, Bill Milvaney, Brian Kremen, Jim McGee, Nan Moncharsh Reiner, Kathy Miller, Marc Segan, Paul Rampell, Steve Brown, Lou Le Guyader, Bill Farrell, Stu Sender, Marianne Strzelecki, Bill Boozan, Cynthia Temple, Ralph Taylor, Florence Brown, James Barron, Eve Lesser, Julia Haller, John Siegler, John Beers, Cap Lesesne, George Oliva, Rick Hamlin, Terry Vance, Ki Lee, Phil Whitney, Mark Stanich, Ed Kelly, David Liu, Carley Roney, Denise Favorule, Christopher Magee, Anne McGrath, Angela Tribelli, Cynthia Crolius, John Steinbredder, and James Taranto.

In so many ways this book was inspired by conversations I had with current undergraduates at Princeton, most of whom are friends of my son's. Thank you, Sam, Mireille, Jake, Rachel, Aaron, Colin, Valya, Ross, Ballard, Zach, Katie, Lisa, and others for your candid thoughts and opinions. You inspire me on so many levels.

Unexpected celebrity sometimes shines a broader-than-expected spotlight. I thank my amazing sons, Alex and Daniel, and daughter-in-law, Tasha for their good spirit and good humor. They make me smile, and I could neither be prouder of—nor love—them more than I do.

And Lucille, my darling dog . . . you deserve a biscuit!

Printed in the United States
By Bookmasters